SURVIVE TO THRIVE

27 PRACTICES OF RESILIENT ENTREPRENEURS, INNOVATORS, AND LEADERS

BY FAISAL HOQUE & LYDIA DISHMAN

Published by Motivational Press, Inc.
1777 Aurora Road
Melbourne, Florida, 32935
www.MotivationalPress.com

Copyright 2015 © by Faisal Hoque & Lydia Dishman

All Rights Reserved

No part of this book may be reproduced or transmitted in any form by any means: graphic, electronic, or mechanical, including photocopying, recording, taping or by any information storage or retrieval system without permission, in writing, from the authors, except for the inclusion of brief quotations in a review, article, book, or academic paper. The authors and publisher of this book and the associated materials have used their best efforts in preparing this material. The authors and publisher make no representations or warranties with respect to accuracy, applicability, fitness or completeness of the contents of this material. They disclaim any warranties expressed or implied, merchantability, or fitness for any particular purpose. The authors and publisher shall in no event be held liable for any loss or other damages, including but not limited to special, incidental, consequential, or other damages. If you have any questions or concerns, the advice of a competent professional should be sought.

Manufactured in the United States of America.

ISBN: 978-1-62865-204-8

Contents

Book Overview 5
Introduction Reframing Resilience, Redefining Success 11

PART I

I Am

CHAPTER 1 I Am Redefining Priorities 28
CHAPTER 2 I Am Shaping My Destiny 43
CHAPTER 3 I Am Moving Forward 58

PART II

I Have

CHAPTER 4 I Have the Ability to Define My Needs 76
CHAPTER 5 I Have a Strong Circle of Support 89
CHAPTER 6 I Have the Power to Be Fearless 102

PART III

I Can

CHAPTER 7 I Can Make My Life Better 124
CHAPTER 8 I Can Learn to Love Myself 135
CHAPTER 9 I Can Be Devoted 147

CONCLUSION 159
REFERENCES 165
AUTHOR BIOS 171

Book Overview

Although many ideas never make it off the page and most new ventures fail, we tend to hear about people when they are successful, not when they are struggling.

This creates a distorted perception of how people succeed. Behind every "overnight success" is the story of a person, team, or organization, facing a host of obstacles that have the potential to shut them down. Those who do prevail share one thing in common, the ability to draw from within to weather whatever comes their way.

Ultimately, there is no one definition of success. The authors have examined the stories of a variety of leaders who faced ill health, professional setbacks, emotional loss, and various other life-changing events, in order to illustrate how each achieved a personal transformation and success. The authors do not endorse or denounce any specific individual, company, product or service that may be referenced in the stories.

This book illuminates how anyone can attain the resilience that is required to repeatedly push forward in the face of adversity.

To our loved ones - who support and encourage us as we chase our dreams.

"The emperor writes: How should you be? You should be like a rocky promontory against which the restless surf continuously pounds. It stands fast while the churning sea is lulled to sleep at its feet. I hear you say – 'How unlucky that this should happen to me.'

But not at all.

Perhaps say instead 'How lucky I am that I am not broken by what has happened, and I am not afraid of what is about to happen. For the same blow might have stricken anyone, but not many who would have absorbed it without capitulation and complaint'."

- *Meditations* by Marcus Aurelius

(as read in the Starz television series *Black Sails)*

INTRODUCTION

REFRAMING RESILIENCE, REDEFINING SUCCESS

WHY WOULD ANYONE want to become an entrepreneur? For that matter, why would anyone want to risk everything to develop a new idea or to lead a team towards a goal when there is no guarantee of success?

This road is often long and lonely, filled with brutal hours, massive amounts of stress, and a large amount of personal sacrifice. In some cases, failure takes an unimaginable toll. Yet some persist, for a few crucial reasons.

To survive: They have no other choice.

To pursue a dream: They want to fulfill their personal and/or financial dreams.

To make a difference: They want to make a difference, to do something that has a positive and long-lasting impact.

My own journey has had these touchstones.

At the age of 14, I began what would be the first of my many businesses: cobbling together stereo components to sell from my father's home in Dhaka, Bangladesh in order to save the money needed to support my plan to pursue schooling in the United States.

At 17, I'd achieved that goal. In the summer of 1986 I had just finished my first semester at Southern Illinois University at Carbondale where I was studying electrical engineering. I would quickly learn an important lesson not found on any circuit board. After paying tuition for summer and fall, I had just $700.00 left. With no family members nearby and no source of financial help, I realized my dreams were in immediate, clear, and present danger of demise.

That is, until I introduced myself to the art and science of polishing marble floors, cleaning stairs and the arena after concerts and games, putting a shine on furniture, and scrubbing bathrooms. As an on-campus "janitorial engineer," I worked the graveyard shift, every weeknight from 12 a.m. to 3 a.m. and every Friday and Saturday night from 12 a.m. to 8 a.m. It was there, in the corridors of Carbondale, where I discovered what it means to survive.

Ten years later, I began the planning of my second company, EC Cubed, with a goal to invent and commercialize reusable software components for B-to-B commerce. We launched in December of 1996, signed with GE as our first customer, and received media attention in every major news outlet.

In less than two years, after raising millions of dollars from so-called expert venture capital (VC) firms and securing top-tier customers, I was fired from my position as the Chairman and CEO of my own company with the accusation that we were "not growing fast enough."

At that time, I was working on my very first book. The VC who took over not only fired me, but retained the manuscript of my book as intellectual property, built on the company's time!

Over the next 18 months, I watched from the sidelines as my company was run into the ground in the hands of these VCs. Their "expert management team" wasted over $70 million in investments and destroyed customer relationships.

While this was happening, I began writing a new book and laid the groundwork for a new business. I incorporated my next tech company on August 13th, 1999 and in December of that same year, my new book was published, the company closed its first round of financing, and we signed up our first customer. In January 2000, we opened our doors for business.

Then the Internet bubble burst, followed by the attacks of September 11, 2001, when the world as we knew it, stopped. Fortunately, my company, survived both calamities. PepsiCo, Northrop Grumman, French Social Security Services, and others signed on. Things were going relatively well -- until the market crash of 2008. By 2009, things again came to a screeching halt. Many of our pending contracts, including a massive opportunity with the Department of Homeland Security, disappeared over the next 24 months.

At the end of 2012, against better judgment, I made a very bad debt financing deal. Things got ugly -- missed payrolls, angry investors, disappointed employees, financial loss, betrayals, blame, and isolation -- the classic mix of major disappointment in work, life, and people.

During this time I began to question the very fundamentals my life - my purpose, my work, and my contribution to the world. What kept me together, aside from sheer willpower, was my family and my moral responsibility toward others.

I began to notice a change in myself, triggering the next phase of my journey. I poured my heart into writing my book *Everything Connects* with my friend and co-author Drake Baer. Rooted in Eastern philosophies and cognitive psychology, the book forced me to contemplate one's authentic calling, creativity, and driving value.

And so I once again began reinventing myself. This time the change was much more profound. My calling, my priorities, my definition of success, everything had been transformed.

At the end of 2013, I launched Shadoka, a venture focused on enabling entrepreneurship, growth, and social impact with digital platforms, thought leadership, and capital. Why begin the hard work of starting over?

As I've pointed out before, the need to survive, to pursue a dream, and to make a difference kept calling me to begin again. However, something else gave me the strength and courage to persevere and build. It was resilience.

The noun resilience stems from the Latin *resiliens,* "to rebound, recoil." As a character trait, resilience is a person's mental ability to recover from misfortune, illness, or depression.

Bouncing back and moving forward also require grit. Angela Duckworth, Assistant Professor at the University of Pennsylvania, and her research colleagues define grit as "perseverance and passion for long-term goals." Duckworth writes, "the gritty individual approaches achievement as a marathon; his or her advantage is stamina."

Those who survive and ultimately thrive in business, and in life, have this kind of grit and resilience. Resilient people develop a mental capacity which allows them to adapt with ease during times of adversity. It is the courage and the power within them — not the circumstances outside — that keep them moving.

In the midst of adversity, they discover what they are truly made of.

We believe resiliency is an attitude; it is your belief that you can conquer anything. It's the ability to go from days to weeks to months and years to reach your destination, defining and re-defining it along the way. At times, it means using adversity to find the opportunities that lead us to our true destiny.

Helen Keller had that attitude. That is what enabled her to say: *"Life is either a daring adventure or nothing at all. Security is mostly a superstition. It does not exist in nature."*

As you read this book, you will be introduced to some remarkable people with inspiring stories to tell. But first, we want to talk about Helen Keller, as her story has had profound impacts on your authors.

To illustrate her daily struggle and uncompromising ability to push through challenges, Keller wrote these words in her autobiography, *The Story of My Life*:

> *"For, after all, everyone who wishes to gain true knowledge must climb the Hill Difficulty alone, and since there is no royal road to the summit, I must zigzag it in my own way. I slip back many times, I fall, I stand still, I run against the edge of hidden obstacles, I lose my temper and find it again and keep it better, I trudge on, I gain a little, I feel encouraged, I get more eager and climb higher and begin to see the widening horizon. Every struggle is a victory. One more effort and I reach the luminous cloud, the blue depths of the sky, the uplands of my desire."*

This may be a revelation to those who only know about Keller from school, when William Gibson's play "The Miracle Worker," was required reading.

In it, Annie Sullivan takes center stage, with Keller's parents seeking out this "half-blind Yankee schoolgirl" to take care of their child, who had become violent due to her inability to communicate. Sullivan's persistence and care brings Keller back to the light -- featured within the play is a pivotal moment when Keller connects the finger spelling of water with the cool stuff flowing over her hand -- giving her voice a new way of expression. Everyone lives happily ever after. Curtain.

But Helen Keller's story did not end there. It was just beginning.

Keller was born in 1880 in Tuscumbia, Alabama, the elder daughter of a former Confederate soldier and cotton plantation owner.[1] A precocious child who began speaking at six months, Keller soon became ill with a sickness that robbed her of her sight and hearing before she was two years old.

Rendered unable to communicate when the voices around her fell silent, Keller industriously worked with gestures to make herself understood. Nevertheless, frustration often set in and with it came tantrums. In her own words, Keller said, she was "less than an animal."

Her parents, willing to go to great lengths to help their daughter, even journeyed to Baltimore, meeting with a prominent oculist to see if sight could be restored. They went on to Washington, D.C. to meet with Alexander Graham Bell to see if he could refer a special teacher.

Keller's parents ended up finding the help their daughter required in Annie Sullivan.

The teacher arrived a few months before Keller turned seven. Sullivan's method: finger spelling the name of an object she would hand her student, wasn't immediately successful. And when Keller failed, she turned to rage-- until the moment she was able to put the feeling of water running over her hand together with the letters spelled in her other palm. Though that moment has been covered extensively in Keller's life story, it's important to note that that day, she learned 30 other new words and embarked on what would become a lifelong career as an entrepreneur and innovator.

Though Annie Sullivan stayed with Keller for nearly 50 years, her student went on to other teachers and schools, progressively gaining attention for her impressive accomplishments. She wrote *The Story of My Life* at age 21, graduated from Radcliffe with honors at 24, and went on to become a well-regarded speaker. During her life, Keller wasn't afraid to take on tough social and political issues including women's suffrage, pacifism and birth control.

She testified before Congress to advocate for the improvement of the welfare of blind individuals. In partnership with the renowned city planner George Kessler, she founded Helen Keller International to combat the causes and consequences of blindness and malnutrition in 1915.

Five years later she helped found the American Civil Liberties Union.

Along the way she captured the hearts of many prominent individuals, including Mark Twain and Martha Graham. Wow.

Keller's accomplishments filled our heads for a while, coupled with thoughts of "how did she manage all that?" and "would I ever have the intestinal fortitude to not only overcome such adversity but to turn it into a platform to help others?"

Pondering those questions, you may be feeling inadequate, even with full command of all of your senses. But take comfort in the works of John McCrone, author of four books and a blog, which delve into the complexities of neuroscience and human evolution.

In a blog post[2], McCrone explores the world of the deaf from an historical perspective. From the horrors of how ancient Spartans would kill deaf children and Romans stripped them of civil and legal rights, to 1770s Scotland and the creation of a special school for the deaf, and to sign language in the 1970s. He goes on to discuss the role the mind plays in "inner language" and the thoughts that lead to different interpretations of words.

And that is when he drops the hammer on the dramatic transformation of Helen Keller from what seemed like a feral childhood, to one of heightened learning. How could she not achieve, he argues, when she had the ability to see and hear for the first years of her life and thereafter had the support of her family to build on? Though McCrone agrees that her learning to read in multiple ways -- lips, Braille, chalkboard -- is impressive, he keeps it at that: learning. Other deaf and blind children did it all the time.

Today, we can turn to Daniel Kish for a modern take on Keller's achievements. Robbed of sight at the tender age of one year, he learned to use tongue clicking, listening to the sound that came back -- the human version of bats' echolocation -- to "see." Using this technique, Kish is able to travel alone, ride a bike, and more importantly, teach others with visual impairment to navigate the world with their ears. He founded the nonprofit World Access for the Blind[3] to assist others in seeing.

We, who are gifted with the use of our eyes and ears, tend to fall into the darkness of uncertainty when trying to put ourselves in Keller or Kish's place. Fear is a knee-jerk reaction when we try to imagine how we'd go about our days, doing (or perhaps *not* doing) all the things we normally do.

But even if our senses were taken away, or if we should suffer some other personal or professional calamity, we can still have the ability to recover, learn, and adapt.

And that is the key message of this book.

While putting Helen Keller or Daniel Kish's story in context, we began to think about the many leaders who, when life served up a disaster, health crisis, threat to someone they love, or fear caused a stumbling block, were able to draw deep from within to persevere, even if it meant learning a new way of navigating the world. Lest you think that each of these people were gifted with an extraordinary supply of self-esteem that allowed them to sail through life, think again.

There is much to learn about the roots of resilience through the stories of courage that have been collected within these pages. We've structured the narratives according to the concepts brought forth by Edith Grotberg, Ph.D., senior scientist and director of the International Resilience Research Project for the Civitan International Research Center at the University of Alabama at Birmingham.[4]

Grotberg believes resilience is the universal human capacity to face, overcome, and even be strengthened by experiences of adversity. She draws from three sources, which are labeled like mantras: I am, I have, and I can. The basic principles are thus:

I AM:
- » a person people can like and love
- » loving and empathetic
- » willing to be responsible for what I do

I HAVE:

» people I trust and who love me, no matter what
» role models
» health, education, and support

I CAN:

» communicate
» manage feelings and solve problems
» seek out trusting relationships.

The book's three sections go beyond these principles and dig more deeply into each of these concepts by highlighting the stories of real people. Though the situations are unique to the individual, you'll find they elicit emotion and action that is easy to recognize and relate to in relation to your own experiences.

Each individual's story examines the essential tools needed to overcome obstacles and seize upon an opportunity. Each also incorporates practical applications for reframing the reaction to setbacks.

The stories you are about to read may also help guide you through a process that can redefine fear as just a signal that something isn't working. Not only is that a powerful way to diffuse a strong emotion, it also opens up opportunities for re-examining your personal definition of success.

Ultimately, we hope that, like the individuals profiled here, you will come to understand that success comes in a full menu of flavors, most of which have nothing to do with money.

Rather, success is a fluid thing that requires a person to be just as flexible and tough as a sapling. It may bend, but does not break when the storms come. It makes use of the rain and wind to continue to grow stronger.

PART I

I Am

"The fact of the matter is that in life, for all of us, we are judged very much by how we bounce back from adversity."

*- Walter V. Robinson,
editor-at-large, Boston Globe*

From Aristotle to Buddha, Rumi to Steve Jobs, Kahlil Gibran to Paulo Coelho, many revered thinkers and talents have said that the path to an authentic journey is to know yourself, to be guided by an inner voice. To be authentic, you must be "awake," meaning you have the ability to understand who you are, what you want to be, and how you want to fit in the world.

Creating your thoughts, following your own path, ignoring skeptics, and dusting yourself off every time you fall requires discipline over energy and drive. Often, that comes solely from within. How we cultivate that inner focus is by taking steps on our personal journey with resilience, which is the focus of this section. An authentic and inspiring purpose allows for:

- » emotional engagement to claim our destiny
- » focus by redefining our priorities
- » pragmatic paths to move forward

In *The Tibetan Book of Living and Dying*, Sogyal Rinpoche wrote, "We are fragmented into so many different aspects. We don't know who we really are, or what aspects of ourselves we should identify with or believe in. So many contradictory voices, dictates, and feelings fight for control over our inner lives that we find ourselves scattered everywhere, in all directions, leaving nobody at home."

An important step towards building resilience is to go deep within ourselves and strengthen our ability to be grounded. This allows us to rediscover ourselves repeatedly. In this section, we explore how resilient people claim their destiny, redefine their priorities, and move forward despite seemingly insurmountable obstacles.

CHAPTER 1

I AM REDEFINING PRIORITIES

"You don't know anything until you've been told you have cancer."

IT'S DECEMBER OF 2011 and Andy Sack is busy. In addition to being the CEO of Lighter Capital, a pioneering revenue-based financing provider, he is managing Founders' Co-Op, a seed stage fund, and presiding over TechStars Seattle where he mentors founders in the hope of hatching a host of successful startups like Vizify and Bizible Marketing Analytics.

Days filled with meetings are the norm as Sack shares the advice and experience he earned from co-founding three successful technology companies — Kefta, Abuzz, which was acquired by New York Times Digital in 1999, and Firefly Network, an internet personalization technology which was acquired by Microsoft. What Andy Sack doesn't know is that none of the knowledge he's amassed thus far will prepare him for dealing with what is coming next.

The Story

Just before the holidays, Sack had what he calls a "tense meeting" with board members at Lighter Capital. The business was doing well, he says, but the investors weren't happy. As CEO, it was his responsibility to figure out a new strategy. Sack was mulling this over when he noticed he was having pain in his testicle. His wife advised him to have it looked at, but the pain dissipated so Sack just kept going about his days without giving it much thought.

"Three weeks later the pain is back and my left nut is swollen," Sack says in his trademark 'plain speak.' His wife urged him again to have it looked at and this time, Sack reached out to friends to get a recommendation for an urologist.

When the doctor factored in Sack's age (44 at the time) and his overall good health, he initially said it was probably just a simple infection that could be treated with antibiotics. An ultrasound was done, just to be sure.

By now it was February 7, 2012 and Andy Sack was in the doctor's office thinking he was going to be handed a prescription for some potent bacteria-killing medicine. Instead, the doctor took one look at the ultrasound and issued a far more serious diagnosis: testicular cancer.

"You don't know anything until you've been told you have cancer," Sack says. He pauses, then does something many of us do when confronting unexpected and life-altering news, goes back to the events that led up to the diagnosis. He remembered how the ultrasound technician told him to take the images to his doctor. "The tech knew it at the time," says Sack, while he, the patient, was still unaware. "I remember the long walk down the hall with my pictures..." Sack recalls, trailing off at the memory.

He doesn't dwell on it for long. Sack admits that after the doctor spoke those words, he didn't remember much else of what was explained about the types of treatments and other information. Stressed out and overwhelmed, Sack says he tried to think of whom to call when he got back to his car. "I didn't call anyone right away," he confesses. "You know in that instant your world has changed."

However, just as quickly as his world turned upside down, Sack says he tried to right the ship by shifting into action mode. The first order of business was surgery, but in the weeks that followed, Sack was dealt another blow. The cancer had spread to his lymph nodes and would require chemotherapy. Sack says he knew then that this disease was really going to affect his life. "This is serious fucking shit," he says, harsh words echoing the blunt force of his fear of the treatment. "Now that I've been through it, it is justifiable," he adds.

Though thoughts of work were far from his mind during the rush between the diagnosis, surgery, and the doctor's recommendation to administer chemo, Sack points out that he had exactly four days to clear his slate of pressing business before starting treatments. "It's a different kind of deadline," Sack quips, although one he believes provided a lot of clarity. "I didn't know what was going to happen and that was horrifying to me."

Being an entrepreneur at a seed stage was fortunate, says Sack, because he was able to dial down his responsibilities as board member for various companies for the upcoming three months. Likewise, because the TechStars program did not begin until the summer, Sack was off the hook for the time being. The most trying part was figuring out how to deal with the "complicated relationship breakdown" with investors that had begun in December.

"I made drastic assessments and decisions," says Sack. Selecting a team leader and giving the staff of six the authority to act without him, he remembers telling them, "Look you guys, I will still be CEO, but think of me as if I went on an African safari for 90 days with no cell phone." He relayed his thoughts and worries and then simply told them, "I'm out." Sack says he recognized the need to clear emotional space in order to "melt down."

But that is exactly what he did not do. The reality was that on the days he felt well enough, Sack came back "from safari" to drop in on the self-directed team to consult and contribute. The reality, as best as he can recall, was that while he did offer some guidance, he recognized he wasn't really 'working.' "I wasn't me, emotionally, mentally, psychologically," Sack admits. "I was pretending."

That said, for Sack, even pretending to work was a way to cope with the emotional and physical rollercoaster. "I didn't produce or add anything of value but also didn't fuck anything up," he observes ruefully.

There were days though that would start out fine, and then fall apart. One such day turned into a full blown crisis, but Sack notes that even a trip to the emergency room was an opportunity to appreciate the value in taking things one step at a time, and later provided a chance to re-examine his values.

Leaving a chemo treatment at 11 a.m. and heading to lunch with a member of one of his portfolio companies, Sack says he felt fine until the end of the meal. He carried on, drove to his office and discovered that by the time he'd arrived that there was no way he was going to be able to get out of the car and walk the 25 yards it would take to get to the building. Sack called his mother and then the client he'd just had lunch with, instructing the latter to come and get him in 10 minutes if Sack wasn't able to call him back.

Sack was having a common reaction to a type of chemo drug called bleomycin[5]. "Blee" fever can set in within 24 hours of having the treatment, which is exactly what was happening to Sack. In the end, he did manage to drive himself home where his daughter found him shivering, with a temperature of 105 degrees. He was promptly taken to the emergency room.

Sack will be the first to tell you that going through chemo is "amazing." He mentioned this multiple times over the course of telling his story. This particular incident wasn't so amazing, but it was powerful.

"I didn't think I was going to die," Sack emphasizes. What he did discover was that when your body experiences such an acute trauma, all the mind can do is continue to the next step. From getting back to his house, to getting into bed, to burning with fever and not being sure he'd be able to reach the phone to call for help, Sack says his brain was working hard just to stay present and continue functioning. "It is more simple and urgent than thinking long term that I might die."

In a way, Sack is grateful for his perspective having gone through chemo. The experience, from sitting for six or seven hours at a stretch waiting until the IV fluid dripped into his veins to the rush of fever and other attendant unpleasant side effects, was transformative.

During his hours on the drip, Sack says he was hyper aware of the passage of time. "You know you are fighting this internal battle with cancer and all these people are walking around outside worried about being late for coffee or stressed about their boss and work and you are in total other orbit." From the haze of what he calls "chemo brain" Sack gained clarity with the fleeting nature of that one zone of existence and the importance of loving relationships.

Six months later Sack, is cancer-free and on the mend. He and his family vacationed to Hawaii, courtesy of friends and colleagues who pooled their resources to present Sack with the gift of sea and sand. While it would be nice to think that the Pacific Ocean washed away any lingering traces of his intense battle with the disease and gave him a clean slate to get back to work, Sack says simply, "You don't go back. You are forever changed."

Sack never thought about pulling the plug on any of his projects. Quitting never entered his vocabulary, even though he would have had the perfect excuse to do so.

Instead, Sack says, once he was well enough to tackle the work he'd put on the back burner for the 90 days of treatment, he hit the ground running. For him, that meant making tough decisions that the average person, who hasn't just had a front row seat to their own mortality for three months, might not contemplate. But for Sack, the very essence of success had changed dramatically. "Before I would have measured it in some form of wealth, some kind of ego," he says, "It would not be measured in impact, time spent with my kids (ages 14 and 11), and quality of relationships."

So while the investors at Lighter Capital were waiting for Sack to get back to the helm, he decided instead to replace himself as CEO. It would take more than a year, but Sack persevered, shifting the leadership and getting the company and the investors to a better place.

At one point, he says, the investors made him an offer and Sack just said 'yes' without negotiating. This was a far cry from his old self, who would have called foul and taken the time to try and get a better deal. Before his bout with cancer, Sack says "I would have told them to fuck off. I would have retuned their capital, kept the business and raised money elsewhere."

Though he could have maintained control and kept the entire equity in the company, Sack confesses he isn't sure it would have been a better business. "I'd have 100% of a business that was much smaller instead of 30% of what could really be big," he observes. The result now is that the investors "no longer feel cornered or that I'm the devil, and I no longer feel that they are the devil. Success actually feels pretty good and we are mutually proud for getting through a rough relational spot."

Sack says he is also transitioning out of his role at TechStars Seattle, in part due to this newfound perspective. Sack is swapping his workday responsibilities for those that are more personal. "I have a responsibility to help people with their life events," he says, including those of the entrepreneurs he has come to know as well as to help friends through their own personal and professional crises.

The Takeaways

Andy Sack's battle with cancer left scars on his psyche that may never heal. But, every time he runs a mental finger over one of them, he is brought back to the lessons he learned during the time his body was fighting to rid itself of illness. Shortly after he began recovery, he took to his blog to hash out and share some thoughts that kept surfacing. In one post[6] he wrote:

> *"I learned compassion and vulnerability. I don't assume that everyone I meet in my day isn't struggling with some life event that makes them feel hurt, vulnerable, or something else. I'm aware that people have all sorts of shit they're trying to overcome and it doesn't always look pretty or nice or calm. I personally feel stronger in my vulnerability than ever before. I cry easily. The world and people touch me and I'm happy to be touched."*

Mental toughness comes from compassion and vulnerability. Vulnerability can be defined as the diminished capacity to anticipate, cope with, resist and recover from the impact of a hostile situation. Compassion means, "to suffer together."

At first glance, compassion and vulnerability would appear to be the antithesis of resilience. Yet Sack didn't cave. He carried on with work and life and continues to march forward with a renewed sense of purpose. It is his sense of purpose and self-compassion that has allowed him to redefine his priorities.

Two and a half years later, Sack is back at the doctor for a routine checkup. It just so happens to be the same day he is talking to us for the book. Vulnerability is still top of mind because, as he says, though the specter of testicular cancer recedes further with each well check, he is at higher risk of developing other cancers. This is not something to shy away from. As a more resilient person, Sack embraces the thought that he won't live forever and the end could come sooner than expected. It just reminds him to keep focused on the things that truly matter, so he can keep going as best as he can, for as long as he can. As he puts it, "I feel more fragile in life. I am more aware that I could die at any moment and that awareness is humbling."

As a result, he has been able to be much clearer about what he can contribute and what he gets out of any project, or relationship. "I am still motivated to accomplish stuff, I like playing the game and I have a lot more fun playing the game," he underscores. Yet he says, "Other people's egos and insecurity is just driving [stress] and I am not going to take that on. Relationships and people matter a whole lot more."

I am nurturing empathy. We are living in an era that is continually being drained of empathy. A study on college students by the Institute for Social Research at the University of Michigan observed a changing of their attachment styles through the decades between 1980 through to the present. Though constantly connected or in company with others their age, the study found that empathy levels among these young adults has declined steadily by about 50 percent in the last thirty years.

Other research has discovered a correlation between wealthier individuals and unethical behavior[7], finding that top executives are more inclined to exhibit psychopathic, Machiavellian or narcissistic personality traits, in part because those characteristics are prized in workplaces that measure success based on subjective metrics.[8]

This may explain the startling rise in the number of Internet trolls. Recent data from the Pew Research Institute[9] found that nearly three quarters (73%) of adult Internet users have witnessed someone being harassed online and 40 percent have had a personal experience with it.

Whether it comes from a bad boss, an anonymous commenter, or a discouraging inner voice, we all fight our own personal battle every day. Because of this, empathy demands we step away from that and see the world as another person, to share and understand another person's feelings, needs, concerns and/or emotional state.

When we put concentrated effort in recognizing others' sufferings, it allows us to put our sufferings into perspective. For Sack, it came when he opened himself up to listening to others' problems and helping them when they needed support during times of illness or emotional upheaval. When we empathize with others, our sense of identity is connected to others. As a result, we feel greater in some way and less alone.

I am caring for myself. Self-compassion is about showing kindness to ourselves. It is vital in overcoming adversity. In his book, *The Art of Happiness*, His Holiness, the fourteenth Dalai Lama wrote, "If you want others to be happy, practice compassion. If you want to be happy, practice compassion."

We are often very hard on ourselves. For many, even though it may be easy to show compassion towards others. It is often easy to blame oneself, feel sorry, and/or put oneself down. It is only through being able to have compassion and self-encouragement that we can move forward, day in and day out. Self-compassion comes from when we reflect inward.

I am achieving stillness. When life turns upside down, maintaining an attitude of genuine thankfulness helps us realize what we have. But to be thankful, one must create the mindset to be thankful. Mindfulness and meditation quiet our mental restlessness. Mental restlessness often includes judgment of others and ourselves, which diminishes our ability to fully connect with the present moment.

True presence allows us to see beyond external layers of difference and identify the core oneness we share with everyone else on this planet. When we recognize the interconnectedness of everything, compassion flows naturally. Being truly in the moment allows us to escape from adversity and conserve our inner energy.

Daily Practices

Now that you have read Andy Sack's story along with our discussion of key lessons from his experiences, over the next three days we invite you to focus on these themes as you work toward redefining your own priorities:

- » empathy
- » self-care
- » stillness

Following the plan below, begin your day with one of the three practices. Look for opportunities throughout the day to apply the practice in the context of whatever may be occurring in your day. At the end of each day, evaluate and reflect on your efforts, jotting down some notes on your practice. After three days, sum up your score against a possible total score of 15. Practice the same routine as frequently as you see fit in order to refocus your thought process and achieve gradual improvement towards redefining your priorities.

I Am Redefining Priorities

Part 1: I AM...

Chapter 1: ...Redefining My Priorities:

Day 1	Day 2	Day 3
1. I am nurturing empathy	**2. I am caring for myself**	**3. I am achieving stillness**
Score:	Score:	Score:
1. Failed	1. Failed	1. Failed x
2. Poor x	2. Poor	2. Poor
3. Fair	3. Fair x	3. Fair
4. Good	4. Good	4. Good
5. Excellent	5. Excellent	5. Excellent
2	3	1
Note: it is hard for me to recognize suffering of others.	**Note:** I was able to focus inward.	**Note:** mindfulness and meditation is not my thing.

Total Possible Score: 15   **My Score for Part 1, Section 1:** 6 [sum of day 1 + day 2 + day 3]

CHAPTER 2

I AM SHAPING MY DESTINY

"I want to be the first woman founder to drive a billion dollars in revenue."

That's Julie Wainwright. Three years ago she founded the e-commerce company TheRealReal. It is one part luxury consignment shop, one part flash sale, and one part concierge-like selling experience.

The idea came to her when she went shopping with a girlfriend and watched the friend drop a significant amount of money on previously owned designer goods. Wainwright came up with the concept, put the plan into action and the site took off.

TheRealReal is approaching 3 million members, ships tens of thousands of items per month, and is on track to rake in more than $100 million in revenue in 2015.

If this is starting to sound like a tale out of the "get rich quick" storybook, here's the part where that book gets burned.

The Story

"My life hasn't been so rosy," Wainwright admits.

That's a hard fact to swallow if you're just sitting down to a casual conversation with Wainwright. A diminutive blonde with an easy smile and an even easier laugh, Wainwright exudes a sunny character that is infectious. And she has got enough kinetic energy and ferocious determination to power through hours of meetings, planning, and running day-to-day operations, on 4-inch heels without needing to put her feet up.

Yet, even those blessed with such extraordinary vitality, experience their share of troubles.

For Wainwright, trouble came early. She was only eight years old when her mother became gravely ill. The doctors originally thought it was encephalitis, presuming she would die quickly. But that didn't happen.

Her mother came home from the hospital and life resumed its routine as much as it could in a home with two young artists as parents to four children under the age of eight. But Wainwright says that didn't last long. Her mother was stricken again, this time with paralysis on her right side. The doctors now diagnosed multiple sclerosis, a disease that would have her in and out of hospitals for the rest of her life.

As the eldest of four siblings, Wainwright felt responsible for stepping up and taking care of the things her mother could no longer manage. This was a transformative event for the eight-year old as Wainwright describes in her memoir *ReBoot*.[10] "Her illness shaped my character in other ways, too. I, along with the entire family, developed a warped sense of humor. We found it impossible to live in emotional pain all the time so we began to find humor in the oddest things. Laughter was medicinal and we took our medicine wherever we could find it, constantly searching for opportunities amid bleak situations."

Wainwright would continue finding humor as well as step up throughout her life, most notably when she took over as CEO of the struggling software company, Berkeley Systems. It was a time, she says, she finally felt "Like I was in control of my own destiny."

While she was at the helm of Berkeley Systems, the company launched its most successful product, a game called You Don't Know Jack, which would go on to sell nearly 10 million units. That windfall preceded the sale of the company, but Wainwright was quickly hired as CEO of Reel.com.

Just before she took the job, Wainwright's sixty-two year old mother, withered to less than 100 pounds and suffering from dementia, passed away. Wainwright took up her new role shortly after the funeral, working through her grief and, what she admits now, were the early signs of marital trouble.

Nevertheless, she forged ahead, building the company, which sold to Hollywood Entertainment two years later for a sum that made investors happy.

In 1999 she made her way to the corner office of Pets.com.

Wainwright makes it very clear that she doesn't want to dwell on this time in her life, save for saying that it was "intense." She points to the fact that she gave over a chapter in her book, *ReBoot*, to setting the record straight on the sequence of events that marked the company's launch and eventual failure.

To recount the rise and fall of the company in brief: following several rounds of funding, Pets.com launched and immediately took off, despite the growing number of competitors in the space. In a brilliant stroke of branding, the company's spokesdog -- the Sock Puppet -- got its own inflatable in the Macy's Thanksgiving Day Parade and fronted an ad during the Super Bowl. The company went public with an $80 million IPO.

A year after the Sock Puppet balloon sailed high above the streets of New York City, the dotcom bubble burst on Pets.com. The day Wainwright had to tell her staff the company was shutting down and the money would be returned to shareholders, her husband asked for a divorce. The press had a field day with the news, turning the Sock Puppet into the dotcom bust mascot.[11] One reporter, who was in the office the day Wainwright spoke to the Pets.com employees to deliver the bad news, had to be escorted off the premises by police.

Wainwright sums it up this way in her book. "Pets.

com was a very public failure combined with the dissolution of my marriage and entering midlife, [which] left me in a place where all I saw were limitations and the things I didn't have."

It would take a while; several years in fact, to get to the place where she was ready to start over and do something she loved.

In the interim, Wainwright confesses that she felt lost and had to dig deep to find the strength to carry on. The first thing she did was lay aside the worry that accompanies the next thing. "I wanted to heal," she underscores, "That wasn't about doing, it was about taking care of my own creativity and my soul in many ways."

That meant a return to her artistic roots bestowed on her by her artist parents. Wainwright says she has always loved drawing and painting. In addition to taking art classes, she became a supporter of the arts community by contributing and serving on art organization boards and attending shows and the theater more often. "It was a delightful way to nourish myself," she contends.

Though watching her mother suffer and eventually die from complications of multiple sclerosis was crucial in shaping her perspective on failed businesses, her father, who is approaching 80 years of age, still inspires her with his creative work ethic. In "retirement" from his own firm, Wainwright says he continues to work designing women's shoes. "He draws shoes all day long," she says, "And he is excited about it every day."

Wainwright says she still gets a charge just seeing the way he looks at things. Although she admits he looks every bit his age physically, Wainwright says her father's energy is contagious. "He has an incredibly interesting, associative mind that can take the mundane and make it magic," she says. "Harnessing that power was healthier to me and helped me bounce back in a way that was incredibly positive."

Still, it took a while to get from working for others to striking out on her own again. "I could have done this years ago, and I didn't because I kept thinking I have more to learn, more to learn from other people, other jobs," she reflects. "I don't think I was gutsy enough." Wainwright says that she has observed how women, in particular, tend to beat themselves up too much about qualifications and mental preparedness before taking on a challenge. "I am guilty of it," she confesses, adding quickly, "Or I was, I'm not anymore."

With the benefit of years, Wainwright can now say there is "something really wonderful [about] failing publicly." It began to dawn on her that despite the fact that she didn't do anything unethical, tech journalists would continue to beat Pets.com's dead horse any chance they could. One high profile reporter was particularly scathing, but Wainwright chalks it up to his inexperience with her side of the business. "[This person] couldn't manage their way out of a paper bag," she contends, and she soon realized that the reports were simply churned out to fill a continued need for stories. "You have to let that stuff go," she says.

With that, Wainwright discovered that she wasn't being true to herself in taking on the paid work she did in those ensuing years. "The thing I realized pretty clearly is that I love creating businesses," she says, "And it was up to me to create my own destiny."

Beyond the basic desire to run her own show, Wainwright insists that she arrived at this place after taking an honest ("some would say harsh," she points out) look at herself in the context of the current iteration of the tech industry in Silicon Valley.

"You have a woman" Wainwright begins. "You have a woman over 50 with a big notable company that became a symbol for the dotcom failure. Legitimate or not, that is what happened," she explains. "So my opportunity for working with anyone was zero." A self-professed high-energy and relentless individual who relishes working out problems, Wainwright nevertheless predicted that "all the normal doors would be shut" in a landscape littered with 20-something year old male computer scientists and engineers.

On a walk with a girlfriend, Wainwright recalls pronouncing, "I need to do something and I want to do something great." After that, she says, "I just got on with it, and I never gave [the negative aspects] another thought."

By then, she recognized that she could have done this years before. But that didn't matter anymore. Wainwright immediately set out to explore the concept of TheRealReal and to see what it would take to get people's unused luxury goods out of their closets and into a selling platform.

Between metrics, market studies, and revenue models -- the latter was key as she didn't see the point of starting something that didn't generate revenue immediately -- Wainwright had a hunch that if TheRealReal launched quickly and executed properly, the business would be hers to win. Judging by the numbers, she's making good on that intuition.

The Takeaways

If there is one central theme that emerges in Julie Wainwright's story, it is her innate focus on navigating her life on her own terms. As she tells it: "I think it comes down to being reminded over and over again that no one is going to hand you your life and your destiny. You get up every morning and create it."

This sentiment or ability is a commonality among resilient people. On the surface, it is difficult to understand how you can control destiny when the very nature of adversity takes away control. We believe it comes from three core concepts:

I am able to guide my destiny. As humans, our instincts are to fight bitterly against adversity. The most resilient among us will often find a way to fight adversity by embracing it. Wainwright was only 8 years old when her mother was diagnosed with MS. Yet, she is one of those people who believes that life has dealt the lessons she needed to become the resilient person she is today.

It is here that Wainwright interjects a story about a prominent female banker who confessed that her dedication to work was responsible for her family falling apart. "You just want to say, 'This isn't about your work. It is your choice, every single day. I'm sorry you woke up at 50 and found your life was ruined. But you were the only participant in that journey,'" Wainwright explains. "I think the challenge for anyone is to understand yourself and what you really want. You create your destiny every day, even when you are winning and you have to be conscious about your decisions," she adds.

To jumpstart the process, Wainwright says, it helps to look around. "If you do a comparison, most [startups] aren't that good of a business or maybe they are really good," she posits. "They all just did it. They learned by listening to whatever customer they were serving, growing the business and moving forward."

Wainwright maintains that startup founders learn by mistakes and make the conscious decision not to wallow. "Some of that is a product of the craziness of youth," she admits, "They didn't know what they didn't know, they just threw themselves into this void and it worked out."

Still, she says, "You put yourself out there and there is this incredible energy. You never do it in isolation. If it doesn't succeed, it's distressing because you let a whole chain of people down. If you have any conscience, it will weigh on you heavily. But you can't let it weigh you totally down."

Once we accept our situation and let go of the outcome, it allows us to adapt and even thrive in the face of adversity. "It comes down to mental toughness," Wainwright explains, "How are we going to act and how are we going to react. These things add up to our life."

The challenge for anyone is to understand themselves and what they really want. Have a personal conversation about that. Ask yourself what you would most desire. Then decide what steps it will take to get there. We create our destiny every day by being conscious about our decisions, how they will affect ourselves and others, and still be able to summon the courage to continue moving forward.

I am able to manifest my success. Destiny results from intention. Our spiritual will can be something that drives us to do what seems impossible. According to quantum physics, our thoughts have a frequency and a corresponding unique vibration that attracts similar frequencies into our lives. Because of this, negative thinking attracts negative energy and positive thinking attracts positive energy. At the start of any new endeavor, Wainwright says, there has to be an intentional desire to get on the right path and make it happen.

How we think creates the energy that ultimately manifests into success. If we go into a situation with a negative thought process, then we seem destined for a negative outcome.

As Wainwright says: "That decision to take action vs. over-thinking or over-worrying, is a key attribute of anyone that pulls him or herself out of any crisis. It is really critical." Wainwright believes that, barring a chemical imbalance that requires medical treatment, allowing yourself to worry about the 'what if' or 'I should have or could have,' can hold you back. "All of that is sort of an excuse not to be great," she argues.

Wainwright understands that putting yourself out there is hard because you can expose yourself to criticism. "Really trying to do something great is scary, not just because you may fail, but because all of a sudden it changes the energy of everyone around you and that is a scary thing," she says. "But if you don't do it, you're also holding yourself back from what is possible."

Take a moment at the beginning of each day to create an intention that can lead to success. Sometimes it is as simple as the physical act of writing it on a piece of paper, or even repeating it to yourself while brushing your teeth.

In this way, you can strengthen that thought without the noise of others' opinions.

I am capable of healing myself. In addition to art therapy, Wainwright drew deeply on the healing power of laughter, which provides both a mental and physical release from stress.

There is a reason for the longevity of the old trope. "Laughter is the best medicine," says Paul E. McGhee, Ph.D.[12] "Your sense of humor is one of the most powerful tools you have to make certain that your daily mood and emotional state support good health."

And there isn't any quicker way to boost spirits than smiling and laughing. Research shows that in addition to easing anxiety and fear, it is proven to increase endorphins, those "feel-good" chemicals that travel through the body, typically while exercising -- without having to get off the couch. Laughter manages to keep muscles relaxed up to 45 minutes after the last chuckle subsides.

During trying times, though, it's not easy to find reasons to dissolve into fits of giggles. Wainwright, who has a propensity to pepper a conversation with her infectious laugh, notes that in her lowest moments, she actually had to find a way back to humor. She did this by renting funny movies and making it a point to spend time with friends who made her laugh.

Laughter diffuses the urge to take ourselves too seriously and puts things into perspective. If you don't have someone around to help you laugh, simply sitting quietly and smiling can still stimulate the endorphins, which in turn will brighten the overall mood. Once there, it may be easier to find a way out of a dark mental space and discover a path toward success.

Dusting ourselves off every time we fall requires a disciplining of our inner energy and drive in order to protect our soul. When we are able to protect our soul with energy, laughter, and acceptance, we can then pursue our destiny unencumbered, despite the hurdles that pop up along the way.

Daily Practices

Julie Wainwright's story can be summed up in these three themes:

- » shaping destiny
- » defining success
- » active self-healing

Following the plan below, begin your day with one of the three practices. Look for opportunities throughout the day to apply the practice in the context of your day. At the end of each day, evaluate and reflect on your efforts, jotting down some notes on your practice. After three days, sum up your score against a possible total score of 15. Practice the same routine as frequently as needed in order to refocus your thought process and feel more at ease with your journey towards becoming more resilient.

CHAPTER 3

I Am Moving Forward

"When my dad died, it was the catapult to begin."

It was May of 2003 and Lindee Daniel was teaching at an inner city school in Los Angeles. Though Daniel loved working with kids, she dreamed of starting her own business.

Daniel might have never realized that dream had her father not suffered a stroke shortly after his 50th birthday. Daniel and her siblings were thrust into a nightmarish scenario: to make the decision whether to end life support or to continue to sustain their father with no hope of full recovery. Though she and her sister ultimately made the choice to let him go, Daniel was still devastated.

In the months following, Daniel felt that she, too, had died. She recalls the sensation of knowing that her former life was gone and her inner energy and zeal she once depended on had left her. She says she barely recognized her own face and voice, as well as the new, previously unimaginable, feeling: giving up.

To ease her troubled mind, she turned to travel. Backpacking through Central America was what she needed in order to get through the early stages of grief. Daniel says that at this point, "The passion to do something big was almost extinguished, but not fully," so spending time alone thinking laid the foundation for the strategy to build her plan.

The Story

When she returned to California, Daniel was still mourning, not only for her father, but for the part of her life she had lost. Always driven to work hard, Daniel put her grief aside during the day and returned to the classroom.

At this time, Daniel was also trying to support her sister, a single mother who struggled with an alcohol addiction. The two sisters and the child were living together until the situation became difficult for Daniel.

It was at this time that she was coaxed into living with a man she'd been dating for a while. Her heart was wide open and filled with grief, and her dream of creating her own enterprise hung in the balance. Though loving relationships offer a tranquil port in an emotional storm, Daniel's relationship would soon prove to be anything but solid.

Intelligent and articulate, Daniel recalls thinking that

her boyfriend always knew what to say and could charm anyone he met. Unfortunately, there was something else residing in his personality. The man was a sociopath. Science tells us that sociopaths have very little feeling for others, and their lack of empathy, coupled with a propensity to be manipulative in close relationships, is often emotionally devastating to their partner.

While her loss was still raw and her relationship with her boyfriend was on a tumultuous trajectory, she managed to grab on to a scrap of strength that gave her courage. She left her job as a teacher and enrolled in graduate school to learn more about the business of fashion, with an emphasis on organic, sustainable fabric sourcing.

Hyper-aware of her lack of training in the apparel industry, Daniel says she struggled to get her own ideas launched, because in part, she confesses, "I am a perfectionist, and I was still learning." Her meticulousness would serve her well in the future, but immediately, the lack of resources and working, first as an intern, and then as a paid employee with women's clothing company BCBG, Daniel had little left over to start a business. Shortly after she resigned from that job, she went to North Carolina to pursue her graduate degree at North Carolina State University.

In fairly short order she started an eco-conscious line of sportswear (which she folded the same year), began developing a collection of sustainably produced gowns, and took a job at a post-production studio to pay the bills.

Things finally seemed to be moving in a positive direction for her professionally. Yet all the while, Daniel says, she continued to struggle with her personal life. Her journal notes for these years point to numerous occasions when her boyfriend was by turns charming and verbally abusive. Daniel recalls how he would ignore her for days, not responding to calls or emails, or worse, talk to her and feed her a string of lies about where he was, what he was doing, and who he was with.

Between the mind games he played, in which she says he could make her feel responsible for his own wrong-doings, he would be tender and sweet, caring for her when she would wake up sobbing from dreams about her father. Out of this confusion and conflict, he would admit to needing her desperately and Daniel's kind heart would prevail. The cycle would begin again. And again. Daniel eventually had enough. She prayed for strength and summoned up the fortitude to move out for good.

Amid the throes of this emotional chaos, in 2009 (in the depths of the recession) Daniel quietly launched her formal gown and bridal collection under the brand name "Puridee." The concept was close to heart and if it succeeded, would reflect her vision to build a completely transparent and sustainable supply chain.

Daniel's brand would create the dresses in the U.S. using Fair Trade practices of sourcing organic cotton and natural dyes. No chemicals or synthetics would be used and the silk would be made through a process that ensures a healthy life cycle for the silk worm.

Demand for conscious commerce was growing. Shortly thereafter, Daniel got her first red carpet press at the Spirit Awards and the collection made its debut at the Los Angeles Fashion Week.

Yet things didn't immediately take off. "Once the business got off the ground, I was still dealing with a demon, facing new sets of devastation, and on-going life sucking circumstances," she explains. Her boyfriend's verbal abuse was escalating, his behavior erratic and unpredictable. She was still feeling the pull of responsibility to care for her sister and nephew. And with all this, the business suffered.

"Starting a business requires full time and attention," says Daniel. The division between working another job to make ends meet, finishing graduate school, and the responsibility of caring for her sister and nephew threatened the nascent brand she was trying to build.

During this time, Daniel did manage to take one giant step forward. Through sheer focus on her faith and prayer, Daniel was able to cut off contact with her boyfriend completely.

Unstable circumstances and unreliable support systems often had Daniel at odds with herself. Starting a business is a risk in anyone's book, even someone as dedicated, hardworking, and caring as Daniel. Those who aren't natural risk-takers often default to attempting to maintain meticulous control over other aspects of their lives.

Daniel's tendency towards perfectionism would add another layer of difficulty to an already challenging time. Daniel says she maintained a tight schedule, based on her goals for the year. Meeting with friends, going out, traveling to see family, even taking a day off or going shopping ("you know, all the 'normal stuff' people do in life?" she quips) happened very rarely. What took up most of her "free" time was reading up on business and the industry. "This helped keep fuel to my fire," she says, during the times when it was easy for her to feel hopeless and burnt out.

She will admit that this wasn't always a good approach. "I took a lot of time analyzing details and planning instead of doing," she says. Daniel then paraphrases a quote about having something done imperfectly being better than not having it done at all. "It just comes down to trusting that you can change things as you go," she says, "Allowing yourself to have that comfort."

That is easier said than done. For Daniel, it would take an external force for her to really begin to believe she was on the right path. In this case, it was a prospective customer who was looking for a gown that was sustainably manufactured. She reached out to Daniel after hearing about her eco-conscious practices. The two connected and Daniel loaned her a dress to wear at a gala for the

Kentucky Derby. After the event, the woman called to tell her that she'd never gotten more compliments or been asked more times for the name of her dress designer.

The woman ended up telling everyone she was wearing Lindee Daniel. And just like that, Daniel realized it was a sign that she needed to put herself completely out there to realize her vision.

"I didn't ever want it to be about me, I am just about the work," she recalls, "But there was this little voice inside not leaving me alone." She fought that voice for months, until validation came in the form of a red carpet success.

"I told myself, since I gave up several different career paths, if there was ever a time where I saw movement backwards or if it remained static too long, I would let go of the endeavor," Daniel explains. "So, milestones were crucial to keep me going."

As a novice entering the intimidating New York bridal market, Daniel says she gained courage when she received praise and support from established players, editors, and popular bloggers. "Although I didn't come out on the front pages of news, I knew there was something good with what I was doing," she contends.

And, she says, she knew she was still at the forefront of a new industry wave. "I would be the pioneer." In a world littered with fast fashion manufactured under questionable conditions, Lindee Daniel dresses are painstakingly cut and sewn by hand and each part of the supply chain supports artisans in developing countries.

One of her signature gowns appeared on a full page spread in a bridal magazine shortly thereafter. Customers soon followed. "Press and acknowledgment is great, but selling is what really matters," Daniel observes.

Daniel credits her decision to rebrand and develop a stronger collection to show at the NYC Market with catching the eye of her first private backer. "Having a successful professional believe in what I was doing enough to invest -- it was a loan instead of an equity stake -- was a huge supporting factor that enabled me to continue."

An appearance in Martha Stewart Weddings soon followed, as did referrals from Saks, and a call came from Suzy Amos Cameron (Hollywood producer/director James Cameron's wife), who is also a sustainable fashion advocate. "I had the privilege of going to their home, showing her my work, and she wore one of my dresses for an ELLE interview photo."

Last year, Daniel's gowns appeared in another Los Angeles show and were distributed in new stores, which meant 2013 was the busiest production calendar year to date for her gowns. This year, as she continues to add new store accounts, the Lindee Daniel brand began its own Kickstarter campaign and Daniel is honing her pitch to other investors.

Daniel believes the "bones," both large and little, that were thrown her way during the last five years enabled her to bounce back from the stress of emotional abuse and the unpredictable journey of mourning a loved one, enabling her to nurture a thriving business. "If those hadn't happened, I probably wouldn't be doing what I'm doing," she maintains.

And, even though she has been approached by people who want to produce her gowns in China or who've asked her to design for an existing label, Daniel says, "That's not part of the success story I'm reaching for." Instead, she is standing firmly in her conviction to achieve her vision on her own terms.

"Ultimately I do measure based on whether or not my endeavor can be sustained." Here she's quick to point out that in a society that is ruled by monetary means, she isn't using cash as a yardstick.

Something she says with pride is that she has not compromised. Philanthropy and sustainability are foremost with every piece she produces. It is a huge challenge to maintain something that goes against the norm, she says, and crafting gowns from silks so rarely seen in mainstream apparel is a massive hurdle. Add to that a business with a quadruple bottom line -- people, planet, purpose, and profit -- which is even more difficult to incorporate than one based solely on profits. Still, she argues, "I would not want to do my business if that was not a part of it."

The Takeaways

For Lindee Daniel, success is also about making progress, learning, and growing. Like the little bones that have been thrown her way on the road to realizing her dream, Daniel has achieved her core of resilience by taking things incrementally.

Your authors knows all too well about surviving through incremental progress. As St. Francis of Assisi once said, "Start by doing what's necessary; then do what's possible; and suddenly you are doing the impossible."

Resilience can come out of daily productivity. And productivity can come from a combination of our thoughts, habits, and our surroundings. Here are three ways that are helpful to drive daily productivity regardless of our current situation:

I am developing healthy rituals. Repetition helps us develop habits in our lives. Choosing to do the right thing, even when we do not feel like it, creates good habits. Mastery follows, coming from an enthusiastic and devoted practice. As a very basic example, waking up at the same time creates predictability, the structure of which allows for sustainable daily productivity.

In this way, we gain the strength and control needed to stick to a path and fight adversity. As Daniel says, "I was the queen of scheduling. Down to the minute at times."

Yet, she eventually realized that flexibility was important, so she now keeps a "road map," even though it is just in pencil.

Her routine has become a calm space in the center of days where long hours are filled with a range of tasks, from sewing and fittings to presenting to new clients. To cope with the unpredictability and intensity, Daniel says, "I start every morning with prayer and devotion time." Beyond that, she's a believer in getting up early, taking a shower, and reporting to work, "just like you would if you were working for someone else." She acknowledges that some people might be night owls and do their best work then. However, "for me, success hinges on maximizing the early hours of each day."

I am finding balance. When we face major challenges in life, we often think we need to work harder and longer in order to overcome our hurdles. Working longer hours, especially when we are tired, actually makes us less productive.

There have been hundreds of studies done on the need for and benefits of sleep, naps, and frequent rests throughout the day. Jennifer Turgiss, coauthor of the Virgin Pulse Institute's study on sleep, warns, "Showing up to work sleep deprived can be the equivalent of showing up to work intoxicated."[13]

Likewise, to be productive, we have to have an adequate amount of nourishment. Daniel says meal planning in advance of a crazy day helps balance her out. "If it was going to be an 18-hour long day away from home, [I'd make] sure I had healthy food or that I would have access to it. Or getting up extra early to make a power smoothie and pack a lunch."

If we want to be more resilient, we need to spend time working toward achieving balance in all parts of our lives. That includes carving out time to eat and rest, which, while they may feel like small derailments on the road to achieving a goal, are actually a guarantee that we will have the stamina to overcome hurdles in a positive and productive way.

I am achieving small goals every day. Being overwhelmed with too many things to do at once is a choice. This may sound counterintuitive, but the fewer tasks we try to do, the more effectively we tackle the tasks at hand.

Most importantly, it helps to focus on one task at a time. Multitasking increases the possibility of mistakes, which decreases productivity. When we perform too many activities at one time, it usually increases our stress levels.

Says Daniel: "I was juggling so much at such a rapid pace, that the to-do list accomplishment allows [me] to look and say today was a successful day, or if these things were not checked off -- why? It is a constant analysis on a daily basis that is really what did matter, focusing on the small stuff helps you focus on the big picture."

She also found that mentally removing "chores" such as laundry, dishes in the sink, and other basic maintenance was difficult, but necessary, in order to stay on track and continue to grow her business.

To quote Daniel, "The big picture can seem so daunting and often makes you immobile, like paralysis by analysis. Sometimes all you can do is focus on your daily tasks, but you can't do that without some greater vision helping you hone in and focus, especially when battling the feeling of defeat that can creep in constantly. I say, for today, let me just get these done."

Resilience is like a muscle, the more you train it, the better it will perform. And to achieve performance for the long haul, we need to make incremental progress every day.

Daily Practices

Lindee Daniel's story gives us insight into:
- » daily rituals
- » finding personal balance
- » achieving incremental goals

Following the plan below, begin your day with one of the three practices. Look for opportunities throughout the day to apply the practice in the context of your day. At the end of each day, remember to evaluate and reflect on your efforts and write down some thoughts about your progress. After three days, sum up your score against a possible total score of 15. Practice these mantras as often as you can to change negative energy and bad habits and move forward incrementally.

Part 1: I AM...		
Chapter 3: ...Moving Forward:		
Day 1	**Day 2**	**Day 3**
1. I am developing healthy rituals	2. I am finding balance	3. I am achieving small goals every day
Score:	**Score:**	**Score:**
1. Failed	1. Failed	1. Failed x
2. Poor x	2. Poor x	2. Poor
3. Fair	3. Fair	3. Fair
4. Good	4. Good	4. Good
5. Excellent	5. Excellent	5. Excellent
2	2	1
Note: *it is hard for me to do the same thing every morning.*	**Note:** *I am addicted to my electronic devices.*	**Note:** *I am juggling too many things at once.*

Total Possible Score: 15   **My Score for Part 1, Section 1:** 5 [sum of day 1 + day 2 + day 3]

PART II

I HAVE

As we have already seen in Section One of this book, developing resilience is a personal journey. People do not all react in the same way to traumatic and stressful life events. However, the ability to constantly get up again, in part, requires a support system made up of strong relationships and role models as well as structure and rules that begin at home.

The people we surround ourselves with can make the difference between our failure and success. It is important to avoid people who bring us down, waste our time, take us backward, and have no interest in our struggles. While we cannot always avoid them, at a minimum we can choose not to allow them to weaken us. Sometimes, the right companion shows up through the serendipity of a chance encounter.

It's not only who we surround ourselves with that matters, but also how we interact with them. And, how we interact with others, begins with understanding our own needs.

Perseverance and trust in our ability to work our way around our obstacles comes from:

- » our ability to define our true needs
- » the way we choose our companions
- » our process of overcoming our fear

In *As a Man Thinketh*, James Allen wrote, "Thoughts of doubt and fear never accomplish anything, and never can. They always lead to failure. Purpose, energy, power to do, and all strong thoughts cease when doubt and fear creep in. Self-control is strength. Right thought is mastery. Calmness is power." To build resilience, our journey should be guided by a plan, a strategy that we consider likely to work well for each of us. In this section, we explore how resilient people define their needs, create support systems, and overcome fear to continue their journey.

CHAPTER 4

I HAVE THE ABILITY TO DEFINE MY NEEDS

"If you put in your best and make the best decisions you can, is it really failing if it doesn't work out?"

It happened on the street approaching a yellow light.

Brent Daily's then-fiancée was driving him to work. Instead of insisting that she put the pedal to the metal so he wouldn't waste another minute idling on the way to the office, Daily recalls being relieved and grateful for those few extra minutes he wouldn't have to spend at a company where he was struggling to fit in. And this was the sign that he needed to take action.

But it took a while to get there. We've all experienced work situations where we've been the odd one out. But this took a self-professed, "fan boy of company culture" by surprise and would eventually lead to a breaking point.

The Story

You see, Daily wasn't just an avid student of what

makes teams click and their companies successful, he held an MBA from Stanford's Graduate School of Business and had gone on to work at Yahoo!, where he became an "intrapreneur."

Within the auspices of the company, Daily put together a team that took Yahoo! Green, the channel that serves up news, ideas, and discussion about environmental issues, from concept to launch in fewer than 100 days.

"I've always considered myself to be fairly intuitive," asserts Daily, so he was confident going in for an interview with the executive team of one of Colorado's hottest tech startups, then called Me.dium, that he'd be able to see whether the culture was a good fit for his skills.[14] He'd soon find out that he wasn't as much of an expert as he'd thought.

Lauded by Tech Stars founder and CEO David Cohen, Me.dium purported to gather social data from users' browsing habits in real time and turn it into a mechanism for personalized discovery. It had already received investment from prominent venture capital firms.

Daily found the interviews "excellent," and soon found himself hired as employee "49" of the rapidly growing startup. As director of marketing, Daily's first day passed uneventfully. But something happened on day two that made him start questioning his decision. At a meeting in the conference room, which included executive team members as well as a peer group, one of the co-founders was locked in a yelling match, replete with f-bombs and name calling, with the CEO over a difference of opinion.

Seven years later, the details of why they argued don't really matter, however, Daily does recall thinking, "Holy shit, this is not how I go about arguing for the best approach to solving a business problem." The red flags shot up the pole in Daily's mind.

Daily would soon find out that his work style didn't mesh with the others. "I'd sit in meetings and listen to everyone vigorously debate and tear apart the ideas on the table," he says. "How I'd historically 'sold' my solutions was completely ineffective in that environment."

As time went on, Daily says, the situation escalated and created a gulf between those who thrived in such a charged environment and those who preferred a less volatile approach.

"The more it rubbed against how I preferred to work, the less I would open my mouth --because I didn't want to get into a shouting match -- and the less I contributed," he admits. It became a vicious cycle. It would be the first time in his career that he felt he wasn't able to contribute at all, much less to his personal standards.

Daily points out that the company had other issues, too. One of the biggest, according to him, was the lack of a clear vision. (The company eventually shut down its real-time search portal and pivoted, becoming an ad network that was eventually acquired by Walmart in 2011.[15])

Yet somehow, the startup had gathered what Daily describes as "one of the best groups, from an intelligence standpoint, that I've ever worked with." That's perhaps why, despite his growing disappointment and deepening depression, Daily's "savior complex" set in. "I was spending all my time in a coffee shop across the street helping my peers get other positions."

For Daily, an exit strategy was harder to come by. That's because he was about to go through one of life's biggest changes: marriage. "I did have those moments of thinking it was just me and tried to blend in," he says. Blaming himself was a natural inclination for Daily. So for the first third of his tenure, he dealt with it.

Thankfully, Daily had a group of coworkers he really enjoyed being around. In hindsight, he says, they too, were part of the reason why he stayed. "It was a good learning experience," he explains, even though he admits it was taking from him more than he was getting. The other half, he says, was the common fallback of just not wanting to admit something wasn't working. "It's just like being in a bad relationship. You know it's not working, and yet you continue because the inertia sets in."

But he continued to struggle. "Every time I had to change who I was and filter my thoughts to present them to the organization," he says, it added another straw to that proverbial camel's back. "It got to be too much."

So one week before the wedding, at that fateful yellow

light, Daily asked for his bride's permission to quit his job and support him while he figured out the next step.

With no job offer from another company, Daily admits the move was risky. Although, when he went in to tender his resignation, "The look of relief on the CFO's face said it all," he says, chuckling at the memory. "I lay the blame squarely at my own feet," he adds, "I like to say that I was a brilliant failure."

Daily wouldn't realize it for more than a year after he quit that he was actually clinically depressed, a condition that made him question his capabilities within and his worth to an organization.

What he did come away with, though, was a deeper understanding of company culture and his own place in it. "There isn't a right or a wrong culture, there is a right or wrong culture for me and I clearly found it in spades," he contends.

So began his quest for creating a way to ensure that landing feet first in the wrong environment wouldn't ever happen to him -- or anyone else -- again. That was the push that set RoundPegg into motion.

Talking to Daily is an exercise in understanding his quiet, yet consuming, earnestness. Behind a somewhat shy smile, Daily recounts his experience of trying, and failing, to communicate with his former colleagues, capping it with a philosophical take on success. Skill to do a particular job is only part of what it takes to succeed at an endeavor. The ability to work within a team to achieve goals is equally important, he believes. So how to ensure that companies hire for a whole spectrum of attributes? That was what Daily endeavored to discover.

For the better part of the next year, Daily says he holed up in the public library getting an "armchair PhD in culture and performance." He knew he wanted to base his enterprise on quantifiable data and not rely on what he calls the "squishy" side of office vibes.

Though he was flying solo, Daily understood he couldn't do it all alone. Just as he predicted, no one would be able to succeed in a job without the assistance of a larger group. So he set up a mini support network for himself. He brought together a cadre of startup founders from all parts of the country who gave him 15 minutes to ask questions and offer advice. "It was great to have somebody else say 'I was there, it sucked. Here's what I did that worked,'" says Daily.

That group was critical in his perseverance during a time as an inexperienced founder. He says, "I doubted myself every 15 minutes. I didn't know what the next step was because I was making it up every single day."

Learning as he went along, Daily soon found out that the peaks and valleys of startup land stretch from 15 minute cycles to weeks. Eventually, he says, he stopped riding the rollercoaster of minute-to-minute changes and got to the point of asking himself if it was a good or bad month.

Two fortuitous meetings happened not too long after which connected Daily with serial entrepreneur Tim Wolters and Natalie Baumgardener, a psychologist building a similar platform to Daily's but for women. RoundPegg was officially in business as of May 2009.

RoundPegg's first product launched in December of 2010 without any customers. Daily asserts that it was important in this phase to make the company tangible even though it had a long way to go in building up a client roster. They did this by creating a blog and a website, even if it was "the ugliest thing you ever saw," Daily quips. During this expectant and uncertain time, Daily says he was helped tremendously by the support of his two co-founders. "Suddenly we were a team and that makes it real," he explains, "Someone is there who's got your back."

According to Daily, RoundPegg has grown at 130% compounded rate since 2011 and has attracted $4 million in funding to date. This is thanks to an approach that uses applied culture science to help companies attract, retain, and engage employees, which in turn boosts revenue and innovation. In other words, no square pegs (like Daily, in his old job) standing in the way of success.

As for his own success, Daily gets philosophical about failure, especially with regard to what he considers a big one at his previous company. "Failure is a funny thing in that it doesn't really exist if [you] look through the right light," he muses. "If you put in your best and make the best decisions you can, is it really failing if it doesn't work out?" he asks. "If you use the experience to accomplish something better, is that failure? These two cases ultimately became the crux of RoundPegg."

The Takeaways

Failure never feels good in the moment it happens, but with time, space, and contemplation, the events that don't turn out as planned offer opportunities for understanding ourselves and defining our values and goals.

I have to know when to quit. For Daily, who had just come from a successful run at Yahoo!, it was hard to acknowledge that he'd put himself in a position where he wasn't able to promote his good work.

"My real failure came when I gave up. Now, I had not only failed to contribute but I no longer had any desire to try to contribute further."

The legendary advice columnist Ann Landers once wrote: "Some people believe holding on and hanging in there are signs of great strength. However, there are times when it takes much more strength to know when to let go and then do it."

For Daily, it took a while to hit boiling point, but he eventually realized, "I'd actually become the poisonous employee who was trying to actively find other jobs for those with whom I'd bonded. I was now more than just costly; I was a detriment to the company. I had to go for both our sakes."

Learning this about himself made Daily more able to take the next step to found RoundPegg, with the intent that no employee should have to suffer the same fate.

I have to be honest about my needs. While Daily was gathering the courage to take action on behalf of his own, unmet needs, he says that one of his biggest regrets is that he was so caught up in his own misery that he failed to help a friend and fellow teammate get another job.

Although he was actively helping others make the leap, Daily was selfish when it came to this colleague. "I needed him, and I didn't have time to find, replace, and train his replacement. I tried to convince him to stay," he confesses.

His teammate eventually left anyway to pursue a more creative career path. "This was a turning point for me, because I realized that everyone needs something a little different from the job," Daily says. "The more honest you are with others about your needs and they, in turn, with you, the better everyone will perform and the more fun the 'job' will be," he contends.

Being able to look beyond himself and assess his colleague's needs helped Daily further break the vicious cycle of sabotage he'd engaged in. The Dalai Lama says, "Generosity is the most natural outward expression of an inner attitude of compassion and loving-kindness." Compassion, particularly self-compassion, allows us to stop asking, "Am I good enough?" By recognizing our imperfect human condition, we can feel more secure and alive, and more able to rebound from failure.

I have to get moving. To combat his feelings of depression and inadequacy, Daily tried visualization and meditation. The latter, he found, made him more anxious because he was not able to allow thoughts to surface and dissipate. He would get caught up in what needed to be done and lose focus. Stress is the enemy of resilience.

What worked for Daily instead, was hitting the road. "Some days I woke up and didn't have it," he explains, "So I'd spend four or five hours riding my bike in the mountains [around Boulder]."

As it turns out, exercise can actually break the cycle of stress, Daily found, especially when he was feeling overwhelmed and underprepared to handle the challenges of starting a business.

That's because, when we exercise, our muscles are producing PGC-1alpha.[16] It's a protein that eats up another substance called kynurenine, which tends to build up when we get stressed out. Though Daily's time spent in the mountains certainly helped him process where he was with his new concept, not all of us have the luxury of those hours off. Most of us do have the ability to take a 20-minute exercise break, though. According to Gretchen

Reynolds of the New York Times, the first 20 minutes of moving around -- especially after sitting for a while -- provides a host of benefits from longer life to reduced risk of disease. All the better when bouncing back when adversity strikes.

Daily's story reminds us of what Anais Nin once wrote: "The day came when the risk to remain tight in a bud was more painful than the risk it took to blossom." We are not born knowing ourselves. It is a self-discovery process, taking us on our true path. As we get to know what we like, dislike, and what works for us, it is only then when our life begins.

Daily Practices

Now that you have read Brent Daily's story and the lessons he learned, take the next three days to focus on these key themes to define for yourself:

- » when it's time to quit
- » your own needs
- » how to begin to move forward

Following the plan below, begin your day with one of the three practices. Look for opportunities throughout the day to apply the practice in the context of your day. At the end of each day, evaluate and reflect on your efforts, jotting down the thoughts that came up during your practice. Did you hear an inner voice telling you what you couldn't do rather than what would be possible? After three days, note if those thoughts have shifted and sum up your score against a possible total score of 15. Practice the same routine as often as necessary in order to achieve gradual clarity about your needs and how best to meet them.

Part 2: I HAVE...

Chapter 4: ...The Ability to Define My Needs

Day 1	Day 2	Day 3
1. I have to know when to quit	2. I have to be honest about my needs	3. I have to get moving
Score:	Score:	Score:
1. Failed	1. Failed	1. Failed ✗
2. Poor ✗	2. Poor	2. Poor
3. Fair	3. Fair ✗	3. Fair
4. Good	4. Good	4. Good
5. Excellent	5. Excellent	5. Excellent
2	3	1
Note: *it is hard for me to adopt new ways.*	**Note:** *it is hard for me to acknowledge what makes me happy.*	**Note:** *I don't know how to begin.*

Total Possible Score: 15   **My Score for Part 1, Section 1:** *6* [sum of day 1 + day 2 + day 3]

CHAPTER 5

I Have a Strong Circle of Support

"I've never felt like I've arrived."

If you haven't heard of Jodie Fox, that statement wouldn't sound so self-deprecating. Nor is she being coy when she describes what she does for a living: "I have this website with some shoes on it."

The reality is that Fox is the cofounder of Shoes of Prey, an e-commerce company based in Australia. It officially launched in October of 2009, with enough optimism to defy the depths of the Great Recession.

As it turned out, serving up a way for shoppers to customize their own footwear was an itch consumers were eager to scratch in spite of the sinking economy. The nascent company broke even after two months. Shoes of Prey would go on to break the million-dollar revenue mark in less than two years and is currently a global multi-million dollar enterprise.

It is no wonder then that Fox has been an honoree on numerous lists, including Telstra's Businesswoman of the

Year in 2011, and was named one of the 30 most influential women in Australian retail, one of the top 10 Australian female entrepreneurs, and a finalist for InStyle's Audi Women of Style awards.

For her part, Fox cuts a striking figure: tall and slender, with almond-shaped eyes in a face framed by a curtain of dark hair, characteristic of her Sicilian roots. But beyond looks, Jodie Fox is vivacious, warm, and incredibly intelligent with a personality that swings from bubbly passion to poise that others, who are much older (she's 32), take years to cultivate.

So it's a surprise to hear that beneath all the spilled ink on her accomplishments is a story of true tenacity that those "best of" rankings never took into consideration.

The Story

Jodie Fox hails from a town called Lismore, on the far north coast of New South Wales. Fox describes it as a bucolic rural community, where the whole of her extended family still lives. As a teenager, Fox struck out for city, heading to a university in Brisbane to study law and international business.

It was there that she met two young men, Michael Fox and Mike Knapp. The three became fast friends and continued to pal around together after graduation when they left for Sydney, where Fox practiced law and the guys went to work for Google. One thing did change: She fell in love with Michael Fox. The couple got married in 2006.

The trio's entrepreneurial inclinations soon had them kicking around ideas for a new business. By this time, Fox had left the world of law and embarked on a career in advertising. This may be why Fox says she thinks she was the one who came up with the idea for Shoes of Prey.

"I don't think we thought we [Michael and I] would work together," Fox admits, "but Mike and Michael were really excited about online retail," she recalls. The three pooled together their resources and quit their respective jobs in order to commit fully to their startup. Shoes of Prey opened its online storefront in April of 2009.

It was a big risk for the three first-time entrepreneurs -- especially when two of them were still at the early stages of marriage. Fox was sanguine about making the professional leap. She reasoned that, as a young woman at the beginning of her career, this wouldn't be the end of the road if it didn't work out, she could always get another job. Fox says she also drew strength from her bond with her family and a caring network of friends in her adopted city. She looked to both as a safety net that would catch her if the business fell, giving her the perspective -- and optimism -- she needed to jump from the relative safety of a steady paycheck into the unknown world of new business ownership.

At first, Fox says, working with her husband was great.

"Most people don't get to see their partner in a place where they excel professionally," she explains. They'd be at a meeting together and she'd witness Michael in action and say to herself, "Yeah, that's my husband!"

Working and living together did have its challenges, she says. "It was tough if one of us wanted to work and the other wanted downtime," she explains, "Even hearing [him] tapping on the keyboard would make me feel like I had to work." Fox readily admits she pushed her own limits, without prompting from her spouse. This had a dual effect. On the one hand, she could see the results of working long hours as Shoes of Prey continued to grow. On the other, it left her depleted and overwhelmed.

Two years in, it wasn't just the work and downtime balance that was off. Fox says they both recognized the honeymoon was over and their marriage had significant challenges. This was early in 2011, coincidentally, about the time they began considering raising their first round of funding.

For several months, Fox says, the couple "tried everything," including counseling and making special time for each other. They were still working really hard to build Shoes of Prey as well, but the labor they put in to their relationship wasn't having the same effect on their marriage.

This split effort was becoming increasingly difficult. At work, Fox had to lay aside whatever mental strife she was battling at home. She was witnessing the cold reality that the vows she and Michael had made to bind themselves to each other until death were unraveling a bit more each day. In the evenings, the two continued to hash through their issues.

The boundaries between their working relationship and their marriage continued to shift until Fox reached a breaking point.

She recalls having a very significant conversation with her husband, the kind that lasted all through the night and on into the next morning. A self-professed, highly emotional person, Fox was overwrought and worn out by the time the sun rose. Unfortunately, she had a media interview scheduled that day. All the makeup and chic clothing in the world couldn't cover up the fact that she was devastated. "I completely bombed it," she admits, "I had nothing left to give."

After the interview was over, Fox realized she had let the emotional toll of her rocky marriage get the better of her. "It was the one time it affected the business in a way that was not cool," she observes. From then on, Fox maintains, she made a more focused effort on keeping their personal upheaval separate from the business of Shoes of Prey.

It helped that the company was doing well. In June of 2012, a group of investors, including BridgeLane Capital and CrunchFund, awarded Shoes of Prey $3 million in a Series A round of funding. "That was a really positive time in the business," Fox recalls.

The marriage didn't fare as well. It completely fell apart a few months later when the couple decided to separate. Around this time, Fox says, her anxiety and depression escalated. She actively sought tools to cope and eventually did require medication.

Medication can smooth the highs and lows of anxiety, but it can't take away the reality that the spouse she thought she'd spend the rest of her life with, was not only leaving, he would still be sitting at the same conference table in their offices and she would still have to face him every day.

But she had learned her lesson and remained fiercely protective of the business she co-founded. "You have to leave [your emotions] at the door and put your game face on," Fox says, to explain how she kept going, "I didn't bring any of it to work."

That didn't mean she wasn't facing her internal troubles. One thing Fox says she learned through this time was the importance of identifying the source of anxiety and depression and dealing with it, much the same way one would seek out the pain point in a user experience, get to the bottom of it, and work to iterate until it's solved.

Despite her leaning toward optimism, Fox realizes that painting positive platitudes over the real issues isn't a sustainable solution for personal or professional well-being. That's especially true in the darkest moments when nothing is going right and most people would just want to throw up their hands and pull the plug.

Fox says having the experience of working in a high-growth early stage company also helped her and Michael make the decision to get divorced. "You start to realize how to say yes and no very quickly," she says. Though she is quick to point out that it took a lot of courage to make the break, "We both made the decision that we both want to be happy in the significant relationship in our lives, and the things we were trying to do, ultimately didn't work." In business parlance, it was time to pivot.

Shoes of Prey has not changed direction because of the breakup. In fact, Fox says, everything is running smoothly. Though it has evolved as it has grown, she says, the vision is still the same. The company raised another $5.5 million in funding in December of 2014 from Sequoia Capital and Khosla Ventures. That momentum has carried her through the inevitable dips in confidence and times of uncertainty. "We want to be able to give you exactly what you want, when you want it," she explains. "We talked about this at the beginning and we believe we are striving to create the Amazon of customized footwear."

The Takeaways

During her darkest days, Fox had a secret weapon to help her continue on the path toward personal and professional growth. As Edith Grotberg, who has led research on the resilience of children[17] and whose concepts we've used to structure this book, has noted, it takes trusting relationships, encouragement for autonomy, and a circle of support to ensure a person's ability to rebound from a setback.

I have a circle of support. Jodie Fox lives and works in Sydney, Australia, which is 744 kilometers (or about a ten hour drive) away from her family in Lismore. Despite the distance and the fact that she cannot travel back home all that often, Fox says they are a tight-knit bunch who keep her grounded. She recently told Martine Harte[18] of the blog Engaging Women, "I'm not under any illusion that my challenges are any more difficult than anybody else's, but the reason that I can pull through is – even when I'm boiling with frustration – at the end of the day, I know I have people in my life who love and support me as much as I love and support them."

Yet, when she hit the skids in her marriage, Fox didn't have her mum to turn to. So Fox relied heavily on the support of her friends. "We do funny family things," she says, laughing at the memories. From cooking each other dinner to popping by when someone is sick, Fox says she feels supported and cared for, no matter what the circumstances are. "These are people I can speak to about anything and truly be myself in whatever form that comes," she asserts, "They will give me fair warning about things they see before [I can see them] and that gave me strength."

Grotberg has written about the importance of trusting relationships as beneficial on the road to resilience. She says that trust develops in infancy, when a child is helpless and reliant on others for survival. As the child grows, she learns to trust others, herself, and the world. Fox's family provided a loving foundation, providing her with the emotional tools required to venture far from home, take risks in business, acknowledge when her marriage wasn't working, and change course. While she did get depressed, Fox was able to lean on her loved ones for help. As Grotberg writes: "You do not need to feel sad or angry or so vulnerable if you have trusting relationships. You are not alone."

I have emotional intelligence. In conversation, Fox frequently points out that she is an emotional person. Yet she's able to reign in her feelings and not let them dictate the course of her business. This "emotional intelligence" has been found to correlate with career success.[19] There are a number of ways Fox demonstrates this, but one thing in particular we noticed was the fact that she asked us a lot of questions about ourselves. Daniel Goleman, the psychologist who is credited for coining the term emotional intelligence or EQ, believes that, in addition to being self-aware, curiosity about others is a marker of high EQ and creativity. (Fox is Shoes of Prey's chief creative officer.)

That doesn't mean she always defers to others. Fox asserts that she is equally at ease with taking advice as she is in offering her own. "I wouldn't beat my chest, but I am always comfortable [with] sharing my experiences," she says. Doing this, Fox has found, makes her approachable and encourages others to share as well.

I have the ability to stay in the moment. Mindfulness is a recurring theme among those who are resilient. Fox tells us that she has learned to be mindful about her wins. At this point, it's important to remember not to spoil the moment. "We are sometimes so far ahead, thinking what we could have done better," she explains, instead of being present and appreciating what is there in the present.

According to a study on mindfulness meditation[20], "the nonjudgmental awareness of experiences in the present moment produces beneficial effects on well-being, ameliorating psychiatric and stress-related symptoms." In other words, staying in the moment is good for you, and mental multi-tasking does not help solve problems any faster -- or build resilience. Yet, as Jon Kabat-Zinn has written: "The challenge is twofold: first to bring awareness to our moments as best we can, in even little and fleeting ways. Second, to sustain our awareness and come to know it better and live inside its larger, never-diminished wholeness." This isn't easy and it takes practice. But the benefits are real, he asserts. "When we do, we see thoughts liberate themselves, even in the midst of sorrow, as when we reach out and touch a soap bubble. Puff. It is gone. We see sorrow liberate itself, even as we act to soothe it in others and rest in the poignancy of what is."[21]

Whether the experience is painful, as in the case of Fox's divorce, or celebratory, as it is with her business' growth, there is an opportunity to build openness, curiosity, and acceptance that can, in turn, guide us to rebound rather than dwell on the pain or rest on one gain, and take the next steps.

It also allows for seeing the world outside of our own heads. In the case of the funding rounds, for example, Fox says that while she has tuned in to the fact that there is a responsibility that comes with the investment, she has also learned that it goes beyond her and her cofounders. That translates into motivation, she says. "Every day, proving to myself I can do this, but not in an individual sense." After all, she's not alone.

It does not matter how smart or savvy we are, nobody succeeds in a silo. Whatever we venture -- personal, professional, philanthropic, political or private -- we must remember the right people are essential to our success. To survive and ultimately thrive, we must effectively create support structures around us, from family to colleagues, to society in general.

Daily Practices

Jodie Fox's story is anchored by several strong pillars:

- » a circle of support
- » emotional intelligence
- » the ability to stay in the moment

Following the plan below, begin your day with one of the three practices. Note how that intention affects the rest of your day. Check in with yourself periodically by repeating the mantra and noting how your thoughts shift along with it. At the end of each day, evaluate and reflect on your efforts. After three days, sum up your score against a possible total score of 15. Don't worry if you don't achieve a perfect score. Practice these mantras regularly to remember to be present and in the moment, rally the right people around you, and develop your emotional intelligence.

Part 2: I HAVE...

Chapter 5: ...The Right People Around Me

Day 1	Day 2	Day 3
1. I have a circle of support	2. I have emotional intelligence	3. I have the ability to be stay in the moment
Score:	**Score:**	**Score:**
1. Failed × 2. Poor 3. Fair 4. Good 5. Excellent	1. Failed 2. Poor × 3. Fair 4. Good 5. Excellent	1. Failed × 2. Poor 3. Fair 4. Good 5. Excellent
1	2	1
Note: *I don't have anyone to talk to about my struggles.*	**Note:** *it is hard for me to be curious about others.*	**Note:** *I find comfort in constant multi-tasking.*

Total Possible Score: 15   **My Score for Part 1, Section 1:** *4* [sum of day 1 + day 2 + day 3]

CHAPTER 6

I HAVE THE POWER TO BE FEARLESS

"I wanted to be fearless."

Hilary Beard is an accomplished author, who has carved out a niche as an independent book collaboration expert and writing coach. She has penned eight books in the last ten years: two New York Times best-sellers and three others that were featured on the Oprah Winfrey Show. Beard has also won an NAACP Image Award in 2013.

But the road to a fulfilling career as creative entrepreneur has been rocky. Her story is one that will be familiar among dutiful children who do what they can to repay their parents for their support and love, even if it means sacrificing a dream.

The Story

Beard has been an avid reader and writer for as long as she can remember. Actually, she counters, even before she could understand what she was reading, as a toddler she would pick up any book.

In her childhood in suburban Shaker Heights, Ohio, Beard spent many hours writing and illustrating her own stories. Among her favorite books were *A Tale of Two Cities* and *Moby Dick*, iconic examples of literature that fueled her imagination and fed her growing desire to become a writer and visual artist.

The vision she had for a creative career was abruptly shelved when Beard was just a senior in high school. It wouldn't resurface again until more than two decades later.

Back when she was 17, attending an art college and pursuing a creative career was not a practical enough path to satisfy her father, who was concerned about his daughter's employment prospects after graduation.

Beard says she understood his perspective. Her father was a black man who had survived the segregation and racial injustices of the South, only to move to the North and endure even more discrimination. He was only looking out for her best interests, Beard asserts, and he wanted to make sure she had the ability to support herself in an unfriendly world.

So Beard says she pushed down her own passion and instead applied to Princeton. "I was aware of the creative writing program, but my father and my community socialization was such that I had no other point of reference," she says. His message would drown out her inner voice. Beard kept herself away from literature and writing, and went on to earn a degree in political science.

That did not mean she knew what to do with her life post-graduation, even though she knew exactly what she wanted to be. However, it would prove to be a short-lived period of uncertainty. Just before Beard got her diploma, her father had a stroke. She says she had no choice but to get a job.

This decision was fraught with familial responsibility. As the eldest child, Beard says she had a responsibility to contribute to her younger siblings' schooling, not just because her parents needed financial assistance. Beard's need to step up was rooted in her reflections on her ancestors.

Genealogical research became an absorbing passion. Digging through historical records, Beard uncovered stories of incredible courage. "My great-great grandparents were enslaved," she recounts, "I learned that when one of them was going to be sold away from her children, she chopped off her own big toe," in order to be less desirable to a prospective owner. Others resisted slavery and escaped through the Underground Railroad.

In more recent times, Beard says, her mother was a part of sit-ins, even when she was pregnant. When her father heard that his wife was among peaceful protesters, he promptly left work to get her, Beard says, adding, "My mother's instinct was to forge a world where her daughter could be safe."

Learning what others did to help future generations be free was humbling for Beard and had a profound effect on her psyche. "I didn't want to be a coward when all these people made these sacrifices for me to go to Princeton."

Beard says that entering a working world that her heart wasn't in paled in comparison to the hardships faced by people in other parts of the world that had no relation to her. "Some people are living under terrorism, yet they made decisions for something greater than them," she muses.

Beard realized that fear of doing something that was not completely her choice made her disappointed in herself. "How could I be cowardly in the face of such courage?"

In biting the bullet and taking a "good" job, she could at least play a small part of a larger effort to contribute to her family's future.

That decision would plunge her deeply into the corporate conglomerates of two globally recognized, Fortune 500 companies. Beard demurs to name the companies, save to say that each is a household name.

She began to climb the ladder, moving progressively towards having more responsibility in sales and marketing. Along the way, Beard went through various training programs in leadership, diversity, etc. One workshop, in particular, made her aware of something she'd been shutting her eyes to for a long time.

On the surface, her colleagues were successful. They earned hefty salaries and had perks, like company cars and expense accounts. That veneer was very thin, she says. Despite logging long hours, some regularly took Tylenol PM to go to sleep. Others were addicted to alcohol or overate to the point of obesity. Though surrounded by hundreds of colleagues every day, at a basic level, she recalls, "They were lonely."

Beard likens her realization to when Toto pulls back the curtain and reveals the Wizard of Oz as just a guy pulling levers to simulate magical happenings. For all the training these corporations were providing to advance her career, says Beard, "The thing I was being mentored and groomed to do wasn't what it looked like. The white men [executives] in the organization were paying a tremendous price, and I was not sure I wanted that."

Why dedicate all of your time and energy to a job that promises advancement but little personal fulfillment? Or worse, doesn't treat you as a whole human being?

She had already witnessed that cost first hand when her father had a stroke at work and his boss never came to see him in the hospital. "For all of his hard work and sacrifice," she says, there was no human connection between the supervisor and her dedicated father. During this time, her mother also developed breast cancer, but continued to care for her ailing father, a feat Beard pronounces "heroic."

So, when her company said they would sponsor Beard to get a graduate degree, she paused. On the one hand, having an all-expenses-paid side trip to academia to get a combined JD/MBA could be a boon to any career. If she decided to eventually leave the company, she'd have not one, but two career paths open to her. Practicing law or advancing in business could both be lucrative. The security that a six-figure salary could buy was not to be ignored.

At a development workshop, Beard recalls telling a coworker that she had other dreams, but if she pursued them she wouldn't have enough money. "A woman there said 'Hilary, there is never enough money,'" she says, adding that she can still remember the sound of that woman's voice.

Later on, when she had to make the decision whether or not to enroll in the degree program she says, "I had to admit to myself that the only reason I was doing it was to have enough money when I was 50 to quit and become a writer." She was, as she puts it, in the "golden handcuffs" of stock options, health benefits, and a car allowance.

So, torn between the desire to help her family and continue to support herself and her own deep-seated wish to pursue her dream of writing, Beard says she experienced a personal crisis. "I couldn't continue to hear that question about health insurance," she says, "When you are in a corporate culture, you are indoctrinated NOT to know those things." This frustration was also partly fueled by an ethical dilemma.

By this time, Beard was working for a major beverage company. Still young and in good health, she'd always thought of soda as an innocuous treat. During her tenure at the company, she came to the realization that those beverages were loaded with high fructose corn syrup and chemical additives. She felt she was "peddling poison" to children.

"That night I cried," she says. In part because, no matter how hard she worked and saved, she wasn't contributing something that would make the world a better place. Though tired and dispirited she wept but knew, "I was not going to give up on myself."

While she was struggling to find her way through, Beard's internal GPS -- her feelings and intuition -- provided some guidance. She recalls going to a writers' workshop during this time. "I was so nervous," she admits, "but I immediately felt at home."

Having a panel of editors from New York talk to her about her work further buoyed her spirits. "They said 'please send me something that isn't a Terry McMillan knock-off,'" she remembers, laughing. She did snag one editor's card. "I hung on to it for years."

More than the validation she got in conversation with the editors, Beard says she also began to feel that her joy in immersing herself into a creative pursuit was a valid way of knowing which path to take.

This is when she started plotting her escape with a peer

at the company. The two put their heads together and created a development plan. "We did that for work," she rationalized, "Why couldn't we do it for our dreams?"

Laying out the plan's steps, Beard realized she would have to make some radical changes to her life. She wanted to move to New York City, but "just couldn't figure the math out." Though young and single, she went ahead and purchased a four-bedroom house, reasoning that she could rent out the extra rooms if she needed to bring in more money while pursuing a creative life. Disaster scenarios continued to haunt her. What if she wasn't able to earn a living writing? What if she lost everything? At this point, Beard says, she started going to therapy and hypnosis, "To disconnect me from events that had taken place that drove that socialization home and drove the fear in me."

The plan culminated in picking a day to quit. It would turn out to be the day her mother died. Though grieving, Beard contends, "My mother [dying] is not why I left. I just became clearer and clearer about who was important to me. It made it more difficult to go back to selling sugar water."

All the pieces of her dreams and the reality of her life were starting to come together in an unexpected way. As a side project, Beard had devoted more time to genealogical research. In addition to learning the facts about her great-great grandparents, Beard learned that her grandmother had moved from Georgia to New York, to escape the continuing oppression in the south. She eventually became Gloria Vanderbilt's cook at the Breakers, the family's Newport manse, and then set out to start her own business. "My parents were the first generation of people who worked for others," Beard came to realize, "Everyone else was an entrepreneur." Except, of course, Beard herself.

In the midst of her dark night of the soul, Beard could feel herself shedding the uniform of the "corporate chicken." Thinking of her family lineage, where members fought to be free, Beard repeats, "I didn't want to be a coward."

She had planned for it to take three months before being fully employed in a dream job, but a year and a half later Beard was still relying on the savings she had put away (she had never used that car allowance to buy a new car) and continued to pray for guidance.

During this time, she interviewed for corporate jobs in moments of self-doubt. "I was in unfamiliar territory," she explains. At least in her corporate office, "you may not be happy, but you know the rules."

The job interviews were a disaster. Her heart wasn't in it, and it showed. "I couldn't ace it because I couldn't tell the lie that I wanted the job. I would be tongue tied, and I knew how to market myself," she contends. While Beard waited for the transformation to get started, "I would get up at the same time each morning waiting for someone to tell me what to do," she recalls. "All of a sudden I was in that space and lost."

Beard remembered the feelings she had while attending writers' conferences and poetry readings. She knew she had to make it happen. That was when a job opening at a small health and wellness publication opened up. It was to work on the magazine's distribution strategy, not editorial. "The idea made me feel depressed," Beard confesses, but she thought she would do it if she could at least be near the creative department. Then the magazine's managing editor resigned and Beard desperately wanted to take her place.

She passed the editing test with ease. "The next thing I knew, I was their editor at less than half of my corporate salary," she says, laughing at the memory. It wasn't long before another opportunity arose, this time to work on a manuscript for a health book.

Beard was unsure whether she had the chops to work on a book, as it was so early in her new career. But her passion for writing overruled her uncertainty. She also got a boost of confidence from the editor who had given her his card years before. Beard found out that it was his project. He remembered her saying warmly, "You never don't have the answer; you do know what you are doing." And she did.

During this time, she connected with former Essence magazine executive editor Linda Villarosa, who encouraged Beard to work for herself.

Her entrepreneurial ancestors' path was beckoning. She hung out her own shingle right after 9/11. Though the country was in turmoil, Beard was taking her journey, one step at a time. She admits, though, there was plenty of fear, anxiety, doubt, and insecurity to overcome, yet she managed to stay the course thanks to a deep and abiding faith -- in God, as well as in herself.

She looks at her resilience and success as an entrepreneur this way. "I screwed up a lot of things," says Beard, "But have I failed? No. I was quite successful at corporate, and I was only bringing a fraction of myself. How could I fail when I am giving it my all?"

The Takeaways

Hilary Beard's rise from soulless working stiff into full flower as a successful entrepreneur took years of personal work. Beard was constantly striving to improve herself, whether it was through taking classes, exercising, getting counseling and hypnosis, or going on what she calls her "faith walks." All these have combined and helped her bounce back after grieving for her parents' passing. It has given her the courage to keep going, even when she has not clearly seen the path to achieve her dreams.

I have to commit to give my all. As a former athlete who played tennis and volleyball, Beard took a page from the basic playbook. In any sport, she says, athletes are trained to always be in the "ready" position. "You keep your body low so you can be agile and flexible and keep your feet moving," she explains.

As Beard grew her own business, she tried to stay nimble and keep herself centered to be ready to move at a moment's notice. In volleyball, taking a shot required crouching to spring up. "You strike the ball with a specific intention," she explains, "You have to transfer your weight and follow through."

Likewise, when she attempted to shed her corporate persona and start her own business, she had to commit completely. Pulling the plug on a steady paycheck is a daunting prospect, not many can do it as easily as ripping off a bandage. That is why Beard put together a long-term plan to work towards leaving why she was still in her day job. The work of promoting soda went completely against her ethics and her dreams, yet taking concrete steps towards quitting, including defining the end date, gave her a positive trajectory. "What determines where the ball is going to go is your follow through," she says, just the way it does for work.

NBA basketball star LeBron James relies on a similar dedication to achieve in all parts of his life. James, who grew up in poverty with a single mother to become one of the league's highest paid players, puts it this way:

"Commitment is a big part of what I am and what I believe. How committed are you to winning? How committed are you to being a good friend? To being trustworthy? To being successful? How committed are you to being a good father, a good teammate, a good role model? There's that moment every morning when you look in the mirror: Are you committed, or are you not?"

I have to get rid of negative influences. Working with a group of people who leaned heavily on extracurricular pursuits that weren't always healthy (see: drinking, taking sleep aids, etc.) to cope with the demands of their corporate responsibility was difficult for Beard. Those crutches led to a somewhat toxic environment during the day.

Her way to cope with this, as she made her transition to pursuing a career in writing, was a far different escape route. Beard would leave her home in central New Jersey to spend nights among Philadelphia's creative community of poets and visual artists. "I would race to feed my soul," she recalls.

Those times, which were spent with the freer spirits who gave her positive feedback, helped Beard gain strength. At the same time, when she would articulate her dream of leaving her job to friends who were still embedded in the world of cubicles and spreadsheets, they would often ask: "Who is going to pay your health insurance and your pension?" Beard found herself pulling away. "I was creating a cocoon," she says, "Surrounding myself with people who have dreams."

This separation allowed Beard to lay another building block for resilience. As Edith Grotberg points out, autonomy begins around age two when children learn to say "no!" Grotberg says it is a time when children make many mistakes and the way adults -- especially parents -- react to those mistakes determines how autonomous and independent the child will become. "If you were not allowed to make mistakes or were criticized harshly for the ones you made," she writes, "you would have been tempted to give up on becoming autonomous. You may have felt ashamed and began to doubt your abilities."

Beard was able to separate herself from the naysayers because she had taken a big step in renouncing her father's questioning. Her ability to rise to meet the challenge of starting her own business began with the recognition that she needed support to reach her goals.

I have faith in myself and my spiritual center. Beard says she undertook a spiritual development program as she made her transition from corporate life. Pushing the boundaries to discover what was real and what was rhetoric made her realize there was a whole other way of being and knowing beyond intellect.

"I had been indoctrinated to develop intellect at the expense of creative, artistic and intuitive intellect," she says. Staying stuck in the old way of being, she says, wasn't a happy place, but one where she knew the rules. Until it failed her.

"I was in unfamiliar territory with my faith walk," she admits. But there were plenty of signs to guide her, like the failed job interviews during her periods of self-doubt.

Once she started to tap into the intuitive side of her mind, her internal GPS led her to so-called miracles, like making connections with people who would remember and recommend her when they needed a writer for their book concept. So it happened, when an editor she met years before called her up and offered her the chance to help Lisa Price, founder of the multi-million dollar cosmetics firm Carol's Daughter, write her memoir. The collaboration would turn out to be another lesson in believing in herself. "Lisa Price started teaching me what it looked like to listen to your intuition and how that could be a real thing for someone like me," Beard says.

From then on, Beard says, "I stopped planning, I dropped the paradigm and practiced being present." She summed up her faith walk on her website in this way:

"In my experience of working with people who are at the top of their crafts, I've discovered that each of us has our own unique gifts and our spirit can open a path that will lead us to joy, purposeful work and a meaningful life. I now know, because I've lived it, that when we work from our spiritual center, we step into the lane through the Universe that has our name -- and only our name -- on it. We become subject to the laws of God, not the laws of man, the labor market, or the economy. Life becomes more joyful and less laborious, even when you're working hard, as I often am."

Conquering fear is about self-awareness, wisdom, and understanding your strengths -- often in the face of adversity. As we see in this story, we can practice and cultivate a series of personality traits that makes it easier over time.

Daily Practices

Hilary Beard's story gives us insight into:

» courage

» commitment

» faith

Following the workbook below, begin your day with one of the three practices. Begin with the one that feels the most challenging to you -- after that, the rest will seem easy. If fear is something you would like to overcome, it is important to understand that it may take time to notice progress. Remember to set the intention several times throughout the day and allow yourself the space of a few minutes to record how that made you feel. After three days, sum up your score against a possible total score of 15. Practice this same routine to reinforce commitment and faith and develop a more courageous outlook.

Part 2: I HAVE...

Chapter 6: ...The Power To Overcome Fear

Day 1	Day 2	Day 3
1. I have to commit to giving my all	**2. I have to get rid of negative influences**	**3. I have faith in myself and my spiritual center**
Score:	**Score:**	**Score:**
1. Failed	1. Failed ✗	1. Failed
2. Poor ✗	2. Poor	2. Poor ✗
3. Fair	3. Fair	3. Fair
4. Good	4. Good	4. Good
5. Excellent	5. Excellent	5. Excellent
2	1	2
Note: *I have a hard time to stay motivated when the going gets rough.*	**Note:** *I get easily influenced by the negative chatter around me.*	**Note:** *I need constant validation from others.*

Total Possible Score: 15   **My Score for Part 1, Section 1:** 5 [sum of day 1 + day 2 + day 3]

PART III

I Can

In an ever-changing world, we are constantly forced to reinvent ourselves. We live in a world where instant gratification is the name of the game, and the definition of success is overblown. Reinvention is, by its very nature, the essence of the resilient mindset. We only truly fail when we give up. Yet, it is important to remember that it takes longer to succeed than it would appear.

In rough waters, when we feel there is no one for us to call upon for help, it is ultimately our inner strength and skills that save us. We overcome adversity in connecting the dots between our inner and outer world. Resilient people find a way to press on! You have to invent and reinvent again and again. That 'I CAN' attitude to press on comes from:

- » our own effort to make things better
- » learning to love ourselves
- » a devoted practice of self-improvement

The meaning of success should be driven by the sense of our individual purpose. Executing that success requires taking the next step, every day, no matter how hard it may be. In *The Last Lecture*, Randy Pausch wrote, "It's not about how to achieve your dreams, it's about how to lead your life...If you lead your life the right way, the karma will take care of itself, the dreams will come to you."

It is possible to strengthen your inner self and belief in yourself, defining yourself as capable and competent. It is possible to fortify your psyche and to develop a sense of mastery. Despite our darkest moments, it is our duty to stay connected to our core intention. Resilient people reach their highest potential by taking risks that are consistent with their ethos and purpose. They lead themselves by constantly standing on an uncomfortable ledge.

CHAPTER 7

I CAN MAKE MY LIFE BETTER

"I had to stop listening to myself and start talking to myself."

As an organizational transformation expert, Anne Grady uses her master's degree and years of work in professional development and speaking to teach businesses how to survive and thrive by approaching struggles in different ways. Over the past 15 years, she has worked with such organizations as Livestrong, New York Life, the IRS, State Farm, and Anheuser-Busch, among others. But part of her expertise comes from the fact that she herself had to practice what she was preaching.

The events that tested her began eleven years ago.

The Story

Grady was pregnant, but instead of basking in the warm glow of her approaching parenthood, she was worried. "I knew something was wrong when the baby kicked me so hard, the force would knock me on the floor."

Grady went into labor three months early and her son Evan was delivered by emergency C-section. Her worst fears were soon realized. "He was aggressive and cranky," she recalls, "Yet everyone told me suck it up." She had already quit her regular job and started a consulting practice so she could have more flexibility, even though she was unsure it was the right time to go out on her own. But by the time her son was able to walk, Grady says he started attacking her.

Grady remembers how he'd be reasonably behaved at the day care provider and then turn on her once they were alone at home. At three years of age, Grady says quietly, "He tried to kill me." She pauses a moment to let that fact sink in.

Of course, anyone would ask, how could a toddler kill an adult? According to Grady, he came at her with scissors, trying to stab her. She managed to pull them out of his hands, but he just scratched and bit enough to draw blood.

Evan eventually calmed down, but Grady wondered how long she could deal with his meltdowns, which came frequently. She and her husband divorced, and now Grady was figuring it out on her own.

She tried everything. "Specialists, psychologists, allergists, nutritionists, Eastern medicine," she counts off, "Nothing was working." By the time Evan was seven, he was starting to threaten other kids in his class and act out aggressively against teachers. Then he tried to strangle himself.

Life with a son who was severely mentally ill -- Grady says he was diagnosed with a laundry list of issues from bipolar disorder and ADHD to cerebral dysrhythmia and sensory integration problems -- was difficult enough, but she was also trying to support herself and her child with a consulting business.

Grady admits that first year of her consulting practice, when her son was sick and his mental illness was still undiagnosed, she only earned $20,000. Another single, well-educated mother would have run for the nearest headhunter to land a steady job with a secure paycheck and health benefits.

Grady was undeterred. Even when Evan had to be hospitalized for two months, she continued to push through and work to build her client roster.

Grady rationalized flying solo as a consultant as a somewhat easier proposition in her mind than hanging out a shingle and starting a company in earnest. "I was scared to start my own business," Grady says.

Nevertheless, Grady took the first step thinking, "If you wait until you're ready you waited too long." Over the next three years, she grew Acclivity Performance into an organizational development firm with clients across the country.

Evan still had episodes, but Grady had remarried so she had extra support from her husband and her new stepdaughter. She was finally able to write the book she'd been dreaming of for more than five years. *52 Strategies for Life, Love and Work* was published last year and became a launch pad for international speaking engagements. It also provided the impetus to rebrand Acclivity Performance under the name Anne Grady Group.

Life has a funny way of shaking things up when all appears to be humming along. While business was booming, Grady was diagnosed with a tumor behind her ear that had grown so big -- yet so deep as to remain fairly undetected -- that it was pushing into her salivary glands and compromising her facial nerves.

A long surgery to remove it required peeling off part of her face from the top of her ear down to the middle of her neck and re-sewing it, leaving the muscles paralyzed. While she was recovering and had to wear an eye patch, she misjudged the distance from one step to another and fell down the entire flight in her house, resulting in a broken foot. Meanwhile, her husband was having troubles of his own. He was in a severe motorcycle accident, and then he got laid off from his job.

You could forgive someone if even one of these events put them in a tailspin. Grady admits that in those years before any of these crises presented, "I had pity parties. I yelled at God. This is not what I wanted my life to look like."

By the time calamities were popping up like dandelions, Grady says she had already begun to understand there was no magic bullet to speed the outcome of events that you do not have any control over.

No one thing is going to pull you up and push you along except the constant work that you need to do within, Grady believes. That is when she had a 'eureka!' moment: "I teach overcoming adversity, but I needed to live it." To do that, Grady says, I worked hard to choose my outlook and my attitude."

In doing that, Grady was able to redefine what success meant. "For me, it is progressively working toward meaningful personal goals," she explains, because if you pin success on a material thing or a dollar amount, it is self-defeating. She posits, "When you get there, what do you do? Do you stop?" For Grady, success became less about making six figures and more about meeting goals such as for her family to be happy and healthy and for her business to thrive.

But it wasn't until she started using this philosophy in her work, when she really started to shake the foundations of everything she had believed for so long. "I told all my clients to start with the end in mind." This mindset also helps when a goal, such as publishing her book, is not met within the expected timeframe. Six years ago, she says, she was desperately trying to write it while raising Evan alone.

It took a lot to admit that she wouldn't be able to tackle it, but she finally decided to table the project. "It wasn't worth the headache and self-imposed pressure," she maintains, because no one else expected her to do it with everything else she was trying to do.

She came to the realization that not all goals can be met at once. "What I am able to do is create a development plan for the business, kind of like a financial planner," she says.

Working backwards, from five- to ten year goals, Grady is able to make incremental progress. It is what she calls the "slight edge" strategy in her book, small movements over time that culminate in big changes. And, she also knows now that it is perfectly okay.

The Takeaways

Anne Grady was constantly faced with trials, from her son's mental illness to the pitfalls of owning a business. Realizing that the only way through the peaks and valleys was to get a handle on her own behavior, she began to become more resilient. "Most people wait for divine intervention or wait for the answer to appear," she contends, "You have to own it. You are responsible for yourself." That is when her mantra became "it is what it is."

I can be authentic. Grady never tries to be something she's not. Working hard to cultivate a veneer can sap energy and make you stumble harder in the wake of a tumultuous event.

But, it's particularly tricky when being a public speaker, a realm where a slick exterior is celebrated as success. Grady is quick to admit that even her master's degree in organizational development didn't turn her business to gold. "I had to learn," she says, from mistakes, failings, and her own family's trials.

Years later, "I share my story," Grady says simply. "I'm not one of those speakers who pretends I have all the answers."

Grady believes her authenticity not only helped her rebound from each challenge, but also to grow her business. "How I have learned to use these strategies, not only to survive but thrive, comes across as authentic. It's a different dimension of credibility."

I can shift into a more positive gear. Grady says from a resilience standpoint, it is important to consider those people you interact with daily and the choices you make in that context.

Friends, family, and business associates, even people encountered casually at the market, Grady says, "We tend to attract people like us." When she was at her lowest, it seemed everyone around her was negative. "They doubted my ability to raise Evan, or even that he had a mental illness," she says.

"I quickly realized, if I was going to survive, I needed a good support system," she says. "I had therapy, medication, and a coach," Grady explains. "You can't be afraid to ask for it."

In surrounding herself with positive influences, Grady says she was able to start taking better care of herself. Instead of feeding bad feelings a cheeseburger and fries, which helped in the moment but not in the long-term, Grady started exercising and eating right.

"I lost 30 pounds," she notes. Keeping in good health was a necessity in taking care of Evan. These positive steps built on each other to provide an overall sense of well-being.

It is important to remember that these measures lead to greater resilience and not necessarily happiness. Grady writes in her book that overall happiness isn't a feeling that comes from getting something. It is a habit that is cultivated. One way to do this, she writes, is to readjust your thinking about happiness. "Remember the feeling comes in blips. You can actively improve your chances of happiness by shortening the sentence "I will be happy when..." to "I will be happy."

I can appreciate that life isn't always fair. When you get caught up in listening to the inner voices that berate you for not working hard enough, making enough money, or being a good enough parent, Grady says anyone can stress to the breaking point.

One low point came she says, "When I was looking

for what was not fair." That included seeing cute "normal" babies everywhere, and moms complaining about standard issue toddler tantrums. "I was getting increasingly resentful," Grady admits.

From this place, it is easy to get buffeted about by events beyond your control. So Grady took a different track. "When I started finding gratitude, looking for things that went right, I started giving myself reaffirming messages." Then she started working with NAMI, the National Alliance on Mental Illness, and was able to connect with people who could relate and empathize with her issues with Evan.

"They helped me go from, it is not fair, to it is what it is," she maintains. "I could change my reaction and response."

Grady admits that even she has days where she drifts back to feeling sorry for herself. To get back on track, she keeps stickers on the bathroom mirror that say "it is what it is" and a big stop sign over her computer. "It helps to refocus on what I can do to make things better," she says.

Daily Practices

Now that you have read Anne Grady's story, consider working with these three themes:

» authenticity

» positivity

» the meaning of fairness

Following the plan below, begin your day with one of the three practices. As you set your intention, notice how repeating the thought to yourself makes changes in your physical state. Do you sit up straighter? Stand taller? Clasp or release your hands? If you repeat the exercise at other points in the day, record how your body reacts to what is being repeated by your mind. At the end of each day, evaluate and reflect on your efforts. After three days, sum up your score against a possible total score of 15. Practice these mantras as often as you need to in order to improve your own sense of positive well-being, authenticity, and understanding of life's events.

Part 3: I CAN...		
Chapter 7: ...Make Things Better		
Day 1	Day 2	Day 3
1. I can be authentic	2. I can shift into a more positive gear	3. I can appreciate that life isn't always fair
Score:	Score:	Score:
1. Failed	1. Failed	1. Failed x
2. Poor x	2. Poor	2. Poor
3. Fair	3. Fair x	3. Fair
4. Good	4. Good	4. Good
5. Excellent	5. Excellent	5. Excellent
2	3	1
Note: *I am busy trying to be like others.*	Note: *it is slow going for me to create positive habits.*	Note: *I can't accept my situation and I blame others.*

Total Possible Score: 15   My Score for Part 1, Section 1: 6 [sum of day 1 + day 2 + day 3]

CHAPTER 8

I CAN LEARN TO LOVE MYSELF

"It is like shooting something you love."

Kamal Ravikant has learned a lot about himself in the past couple of years. A serial entrepreneur, he had built businesses and consulted for others for over a decade. Yet, his bio indicates that he is the epitome of an experiential learner: climbing to one of the highest base camps in the Himalayas, meditating with the monks at the Dalai Lama's monastery, spending three months traversing Georgia's swamps at the age of 18 to earn a badge from the U.S. Army Infantry, trekking Spain's famed pilgrimage route El Camino de Santiago, and being the only male member of a black women writers' group.

Despite traveling to numerous countries and connecting with hundreds of people, Ravikant wasn't able to predict the extreme personal and professional crisis he experienced not too long ago.

The Story

About ten years ago, Kamal Ravikant was working on a side project when he stumbled across an idea that every startup founder dreams of. He had found a way to truly disrupt an industry that was bogged down in what he calls shady practices and scammy deals.

"It was a really exciting chance to transform an industry," says Ravikant. "A very rare moment in any career."

Without taking too deep a dive into the details, Ravikant describes the domain industry circa 2005-2006 as a landscape dominated -- albeit very quietly -- by two major and very recognizable players. He explains how these Internet titans were making literal billions from advertisement fees generated on web domains that were arrived at every time someone went to type in a search term and made a typo.

Ravikant maintains this typo traffic was enormous and the revenue from ads on websites that took advantage of slight misspellings was in the billions of dollars. But it wasn't easily traced back to the tech giants because they used third party companies, from which they collected domain fees, in addition to money they got from placing ads on those sites.

Though he doesn't classify himself as having a reality distortion field, this kind of arbitrage got Ravikant thinking: "What if this was done in the open? What if we could create real value for advertisers by using code and data to filter out products and on the other end you actually aren't sending the people who are typing in this stuff to some scammy website?" In the end, Ravikant likens his quest to an act of countering terrorism. "If you want to stop it, you go for the people funding it, those who are actually making it possible."

So he pulled together a team of Silicon Valley's best and brightest, including a founding engineer of Netscape, who Ravikant credits with building the very first browser, and the engineer who built OpenDNS. "We had a world class tech team to solve this problem," Ravikant contends. And though he says it took them a while to learn the ins and outs of the industry, Ravikant says they were making good progress towards converting the entire experience for users and the companies who controlled large portfolios of domains. "It was better for everyone," he asserts.

Applications were developed and patents were filed.[22] The business had raised a seed round of funding from the likes of SoftTech and First Round.[23] They started to build a second mobile application. Ravikant had poured his own money in, too. Not to mention, he was working non-stop, with no vacation. He remembers having to force himself to take a break on Sundays.

And then, as Ravikant was negotiating a major partnership, "the whole thing just fell apart." In that crucial moment, he realized that the business -- and he -- had encountered a classic problem. He recounts the parable of the Buddhist monk who comes to a river crossing and there, waiting on the shore, is a scorpion. The creature asks if the monk will carry him across the river on his back, and the monk is rightfully suspicious about getting stung. Still, he lets the scorpion climb on and proceeds to cross the river. And then -- surprise -- the scorpion stings the monk. "Why?" the monk pleads. "Because I am a scorpion," the creature replies.

Ravikant says this dynamic played out as he and his team were building the business. Despite their best efforts to clean up what he repeatedly calls a shady industry and deliver value, he was thwarted. Why? Because, he says, most of the players in the domain industry were money-driven scorpions and not mission-driven like Ravikant and many others who sought to innovate in Silicon Valley. "We got stung," he says, "They screwed us."

What was worse, was that the money was running out. Ravikant's personal resources were dwindling, he'd racked up significant credit card debt, and was running on empty. Still, he says, he persevered in hopes that the mobile application would buoy the team. That optimism would be short lived.

While he can't pinpoint the worst day, Ravikant remembers looking out of the window of his office and taking in the sweeping view of the Bay Bridge. It was late on a Saturday night having a conversation that he no longer remembers. "I looked at the bridge and wished I could jump off," he says quietly.

Life had gotten untenable. Ravikant admits that, in hindsight, therapy would have been very helpful as he navigated these rough waters. "I was too busy," he quips. He recalls days when he was letting staff go, one by one. "These are people you dearly love, investors, friends. I had to look them in the eye and tell them I was sorry."

Some were understanding. Indeed, it was a time to discover who really had his back. Others, such as one investor, were unkind. "He just went for my head and made my life miserable," says Ravikant, who felt like he was being attacked from every side. The last place people evolve into their best selves is in business, Ravikant would learn. "If they have been screwed over in the past, it brings out every single fear and insecurity," he observes. Money and power, he believes, have the ability to make good people inhumane.

Then he got sick, really sick. For months he tried to recover, but some days he didn't have the energy to get out of bed at all. "I was lost," he says, by way of explaining the illness that immobilized him. "I didn't believe in [the business] anymore." By the end of 2012, the company was dissolving. "Sometimes the best thing you can do is shoot the damn thing," he admits.

From his bedroom, when he was too weak to go out, he had another epiphany. It is one he wrote about in his pivotal book *Love Yourself Like Your Life Depends On It*. Ravikant realized that, while he had poured his heart and soul into his work, he had neglected the very core of himself. He began to understand that he would have to learn to love himself in order to survive and thrive, no matter the endeavor or challenge.

As he looked in the mirror and said, "I love myself," other things started to come into focus. Like the fact that others saw him as someone driven to succeed. "I thought that as well until I loved myself," he writes. That was until he woke up to the truth: that he was actually driven to not fail. Despite the consistent the work to keep his company pushing forward, his actions only ensured his task was like that of Sisyphus. He was pushing that rock uphill, averting disaster. "Never failing, but never taking off the way I knew it should," he writes.

From this new insight, came more revelations. There was freedom in these truths, Ravikant maintains, and he started feeling better. "It is what I consider magic," he emphasizes, "For one person it's $10,000 or $1 million." For him, learning to truly love himself was a game changer. "I found a core thing that really matters."

His emotional outlook improved, and his physical health turned around. He found the courage to write about his experiences in *Love Yourself Like Your Life Depends On It*. It was immediately successful, and Ravikant says, became the revenue stream that would help him start pulling out of the debt he accrued while running the business.

He is using those pivotal moments to help others now. He started Evolve VC[24], and has made about a dozen investments in early-stage companies. He is also advising startups, because he knows, "leadership is lonely." He invites CEOs to call him anytime, because he understands how difficult it is to fully share problems when you are the one in charge. "No matter what the age of the [staff], they still look up to you," he explains, "I am only here to support the entrepreneur."

As for success, Ravikant says simply, it's a full on expression of who you are. "You risk your ego because it is so damn fulfilling."

The Takeaways

Ravikant has come a long way in just a few short years, transforming from misery and defeat to strength and security. He is grateful for the experience, he says. "I was 40 [at that time] and I think about the guy I was, I [feel] such love for him because I exist because of him," he states.

I can learn to love myself. Ravikant knows what it is like to hit rock bottom on every front. "When your ego [is] shattered and you look in the mirror and feel like it is never going to end, there is no way out," he says. "You have to reach in and find that place."

In learning to love himself, he had to start at the beginning. "That is the best gift," he says "the beginner mind." From there, he says it is important to substitute all the things that make us feel inadequate with our own unique value proposition. "Yes, it is terrifying," he agrees, a feeling that was magnified when he published his first book. You have to get beyond the fact that you might be poorly received, Ravikant says.

He writes in *Love Yourself Like Your Life Depends On It*, "If a painful memory arises, don't fight it or try to push it away – you're in quicksand. Struggle reinforces pain. Instead, go to love. Love for yourself. Feel it. If you have to fake it, fine. It'll become real eventually. Feel the love for yourself as the memory ebbs and flows. That will take the power away."

"And even more importantly, it will shift the wiring of the memory. Do it again and again. Love. Re-wire. Love. Re-wire. It's your mind. You can do whatever you want."

I can create my way out of the pain. Having some success in business and in life sometimes has the opposite effect on your psyche, Ravikant says, because it can make you fear failure even more.

When that happens, it is more important to take risks in order to keep moving forward. "There's a selfish reason to do it," he observes. "You become a better you in the process. Entrepreneurship is about that."

What it takes to build a resilient mindset as well as a resilient business is the step-up, maintains Ravikant. "The only time for wings to sprout is when we jump," he underscores. He knows it is not easy, but if we stand there and wait, it will never happen.

Ravikant likens not taking a risk and starting again to self-hate, allowing fear to dictate our actions. Instead, it is important to start creating something, anything to work ourselves away from getting stuck in failure.

As he writes in *Live Your Truth*, "If ever in pain, I think the best thing we can do is to create something. A record. Not of pain, but of what is real. Pain doesn't last. And when it's gone, we have something to show for it. Growth. And because it is a human experience, it is of value."

I can believe that I am enough. Carol Dweck, professor of psychology at Stanford, said in an interview, "We need to get out of the mode of self-judgment, of constantly judging our abilities from our actions. If we judge ourselves as we make mistakes, we are more intimidated than inspired to try again. We ought to celebrate instead the act of curiosity that led us to explore, and then try again."

For Ravikant, this has translated into the work of writing his second book. Even now, he admits that *Live Your Truth* sells two copies for every ten that his first book sells. But that isn't important. What does resonate for Ravikant is that he was able to put out a record of his own personal evolution without fear of replicating his first success.

"You've got to put out what is you," he says. "It is the most selfish thing you can do and the most beautiful."

Daily Practices

From Kamal Ravikant's story, we have summed up three concepts necessary to becoming more resilient:

» self-love
» self-expression
» self-confidence

Following the plan below, begin to set the intention that most resonates with your own need to develop as a human being. Pay attention to how you feel when you explore the intention to love your own self. Are you able to say with confidence that you are truly loved? Jot down the thoughts that dampen your self-esteem and meditate on how you might turn those around. At the end of each day, evaluate and reflect on your efforts, then sum up your score after three days against a possible total score of 15. Practice these mantras repeatedly to move towards a more authentic way of loving yourself.

Part 3: I CAN...

Chapter 8: ...Love Myself

Day 1	Day 2	Day 3
1. I can learn to love myself	**2. I can create my way out of the pain**	**3. I can believe that I am enough**
Score:	**Score:**	**Score:**
1. Failed x	1. Failed	1. Failed x
2. Poor	2. Poor	2. Poor
3. Fair	3. Fair	3. Fair
4. Good	4. Good x	4. Good
5. Excellent	5. Excellent	5. Excellent
1	4	1
Note: Greatness is not for someone average like me.	**Note:** I find comfort when I create.	**Note:** I am constantly beating myself up.

Total Possible Score: 15 **My Score for Part 1, Section 1:** 6 [sum of day 1 + day 2 + day 3]

CHAPTER 9

I CAN BE DEVOTED

"I became numb to the difficulties."

Brad Feld has won and lost and won again over the course of nearly[25] years. The dotcom bust that decimated his company and lost an astonishing amount of money, the aftershocks of September 11th, and bouts with depression have taken their place alongside a number of successes.

Among his hits: Feld's very first software company, which he started during his sophomore year at MIT with just $10 that grew to several million in revenue in six years and eventually got acquired by a public company. He started on his investing trajectory shortly thereafter when he made his first angel investments in companies such as Netgenesis, which later went public, and Harmonix, creator of Guitar Hero, and more recently Makerbot and Fitbit. Over the past decade, he has completed 24 marathons (almost halfway to his goal of participating in one in every state).

Each rise and fall has brought Feld to one important lesson: be truly in the moment.

Living in the moment doesn't mean we don't care about the past or future. It means when we make a choice to do something, we focus on doing it, rather than letting our mind wander into the future (or back into the past). Being present allows Feld to rise above adversity and conserve inner energy. But this had to be learned. And then put into practice.

The Story

Brad Feld isn't one to shy away from talking about times when things have not gone his way. In fact, he has been very forthcoming about it in writings which reach hundreds of thousands of followers. Here's a rundown, according to Feld's blog, Feld Thoughts[25]:

"My first company, Martingale Software, failed (we returned $7,000 of the $10,000 we raised.) My second company, DataVision Technologies, failed. And the second VC fund I was part of, which raised $660 million in 1999, was a complete disaster."

But Feld tells us his most significant failure came from a company he cofounded in 1996. The company, Interliant, was designed to provide web hosting and a variety of services including network-based applications for clients who preferred not to develop those systems in-house.

Interliant was officially launched the following year and continued to grow, thanks to a group of acquisitions which raised the company's customer base to just shy of 50,000 customers and nearly 80,000 active domains.[26] As Internet growth continued to exceed expectations, the company set its sights on an initial public offering. Interliant debuted on the NASDAQ in 1999 at $10 a share.

Feld says it wasn't long before Interliant reached its peak. But it wouldn't take long to topple. Just as quickly as dotcom businesses were flourishing, the economy started to tank, popping the first bubble. In April of 2001, Interliant announced a major restructuring to focus on a few core areas of the business. This move meant that 190 people were laid off.[27]

For a short time, there was a glimmer of hope. In October of 2001, a former executive of Interliant penned a piece, declaring the sale of the company's retail web hosting operation a smart move and one that could attract an acquisition.[28] That never happened. Revenue started to plummet and equity financing deals were pulled.

Feld cuts to the chase. "In 2000, the market cap was a little less than $3 billion," he says. Then, without taking so much as a breath, he adds, "It went bankrupt in 2002.[29]"

That wasn't all. Feld confesses that he was heavily immersed in a personal struggle right around 2000. "My wife Amy -- we'd been together for a decade -- basically reached the point of being done with our relationship because of how work was all-consuming."

While all this was going down, Feld had flown to New York on the red eye the morning of September 11, 2001. He went to his hotel and went straight to bed, and says he was asleep when the first tower fell, safely miles uptown from Ground Zero.

Confusion ensued. "No one could find me," and it shook everyone up. Feld says he had a friend lend him a car and he drove all the way back home to Boulder the next day. The next three months were rough. "I had very deep depression," he admits. It would be one of three major clinical depressions he experienced as an adult (another one came at the beginning of 2013 and lasted six months). "It was really hard to get up in the morning and deal with anything," he recalls. "So I just decided not to travel, cancelled a ton of optional stuff, and carved out as much time as I could for myself." Then, he admits, "2001 was a brutal, brutal, brutal year for me."

Piecing his personal life together as well as coming to terms with Interliant's filing for Chapter 11 bankruptcy protection would have been difficult enough, but Feld's problems were still escalating.

As co-chairman of Interliant, he and the other directors were sued $150 million for fraud. "It took us three years to settle," Feld says, but not before he had what he writes was a "vomit moment," upon seeing his name splashed all over the pages of the suit.[30] "Effectively, there was no fraud," he explains, "it was one of those situations we had a $40 MM director and officer liability policy and they went after that D&O insurance." Feld estimates that the plaintiffs spent about $3 million to get a settlement that netted about $600,000.

Right on the heels of this, Feld's venture firm was also taking a hit. "I made a commitment to myself. I had to decide to leave or get it out of the ditch it was in," he says. Ultimately, Feld decided to be actively engaged through the end of 2007.

He is quick to note that during that period of time, something shifted in his mind. "It was not difficult to confront the hard things," he asserts. Instead, Feld says, "I became numb to the difficulties." What had happened was the beginning of a realization that he was spending an "immense amount" of energy on having things resolved the way he envisioned.

"At some point it became detachment," he says. Situations will resolve one way or the other, maybe not exactly the way he'd like, but they'd still come to a natural conclusion. By recognizing this, Feld began building resilience simply by allowing himself to be less wound up with the results. The unintended benefit? "Predictably, most worked out the way I wanted."

Feld's definition of success has predictably evolved as well, in part because he says he is not thinking much about defining it. Most people at mid-life (Feld is turning 50 years old soon) think in terms of what they would like others to say about them after they are gone. "When I'm dead. I'm dead," says Feld pragmatically. "I'm focused on the tens of thousands of days I have left to contribute and to feel satisfied when I reflect that I've done things that mattered to me," he posits, like teaching.

He credits life's rough patches, from a divorce from his first wife to dropping out of MIT's Ph.D. program, with getting to a place where financial and business success do not matter as much.

Feld is also candid about using therapy as a tool to help him get to this place. In addition, the recognition that he is an introvert who just happens to be a very public person, has allowed him to order his energy so he doesn't get too drained.

Unlike some people, who use January 1st or their birthday to take stock of their accomplishments and make resolutions, Feld says he does the opposite of an annual check-in. "I have rhythms for things I try to get done," he explains. By eliminating the need to get "an 'A' or a gold star," Feld says he is able to keep focused on the space in front of him.

The result: "I am doing much higher quality work because I don't feel pressed by all this stuff I have to get done," he says. Much less getting derailed when things don't go as planned or fail in dramatic fashion. "I simplify it, and I am really in the moment."

The Takeaways

Feld says he has learned a lot from each failure, but that perfect storm of bankruptcy, lawsuit, marriage problems, and the aftermath of September 11th shaped him the most. In the space of those years, Feld says he overhauled his thinking. It has informed the way he makes a lot of his professional decisions, confronts things directly, and deals with conflict.

To get there, Feld says he's cultivated a sense of detachment and mental serenity that allow him to be totally present, but not upended if there is a crisis. He has mastered several ways to do this.

I can detach myself from shame. Feld believes that the very idea of "celebrating" failure a weird misnomer that has somehow taken hold in all of the reporting about startups. "No one really celebrates it, that's bullshit shtick," he argues.

"I think accepting it and recognizing the entrepreneurial process [as] very powerful," he recommends and proceeds to tell the story of how one Boulder startup that shuttered allowed this to unfold in a positive way. "The company got a group of people together and they had a wake," he explains. "They celebrated the life of the company," he says, and then they "buried it" and moved on.

The failure, Feld contends, was part of the experience. "But it doesn't define you." At this point it's important not to let the embarrassment over what went wrong get the best of you. "Shame accelerates when you let the narrative take over," he says. "Shame comes from not confronting your fears."

Instead, Feld advises, it is important to confront that fear. Some experts advise writing down a list of worst-case scenarios in one column, and in another, ways to deal with them. The act of recording those fears in a concrete way not only allows you to brainstorm a solution, but avoids the entire shadowy "monsters-under-the-bed syndrome" that comes from not being able to define the boundaries of a problem. As Feld writes, "I separate how I feel from failure from how I feel about life and what I'm doing."

Resilience, then, can spring from repeated use of this practice. Examine failure. Hold it up to the light and recognize what went wrong. Take the time to define your worst fears before going forward and before they lead to shame and discouragement from reaching your goals.

I can learn from my peers. Feld has been a fan of peer groups since he started the Boston chapter of Young Entrepreneurs in the early 1990s. "Some of those developed deep personal friendships for me," he says, including one best friend who was there for him during his most recent bout with depression in 2013.

Unlike what we've written about Jodie Fox and her close circle of supportive friends, Feld says he has always found a group of entrepreneurs -- strangers, really -- going through the same stresses and challenges of starting a business who have helped throughout his journey. "You can take a deep breath, slow down, open your eyes, look around, recognize that you are not alone," Feld insists, "and these [problems] are not unique to you."

Resilience isn't easy for the lonely hero, as some leaders imagine themselves. In fact, Feld says, listening to others' trials and successes can actually help build the ability to bounce back. "Use them to develop new skills, new tools, and energy," he says of peer groups. "It helps you get perspective."

I can meditate. Like many of us, Feld was curious but skeptical about the usefulness of meditation. He began using an app called Headspace, which offers short, guided meditations, pledging he would try it for a month. "Now it's been a year," he says and he's up to 20 minutes per day. "It's pretty remarkable."

Indeed, a growing body of research[31] indicates that meditation can cut through stress and lower blood pressure, boost emotional well-being and increase self-awareness. Within his own meditations, Feld works on not suppressing thoughts or anxiety, but acknowledging feelings, labeling them, and coming back to the breath. Sometimes this helps soothe the mind. Other times it offers solace in an unexpected way.

Recently, he wrote about how his mind wandered

through the notion of narrating his life events. After he was done, he kept pondering the narrative and its impact on his life. "I realize that many of the narratives I create are irrelevant," he writes in his blog. "When I ask myself 'will anyone care in 150 years?' the answer is a definitive 'NO!' When I ask myself whether this narrative actually will impact the outcome of the situation, the answer is often no, although not necessarily as definitive."

From there, Feld says he has been able to take steps towards further acceptance and resilience. He is not always able to keep up the daily routine, missing a day every other week or so. When he does miss a session, or if he is not able to sit quietly as directed, he tries to remember the advice of friends. "They tell me, 'remember it's a practice,'" he says. "It's not that you master it, you just practice." And he adds with a chuckle, "What is success in the context of meditation? I don't know, and I'm not sure I care."

For Feld, the resilience that has come from those events also helps now with his ability to absorb and handle the big ups and downs that are inevitable in anyone's life.

Daily Practices

Brad Feld's story gives us insight into:
- » shame
- » the wisdom of others

» the importance of meditation

Following the plan below, begin your day with one of the three practices, understanding that what appears to be the most difficult concept will often take the longest to shift within your mind. Take time to set your intention periodically throughout the day, and note how the most challenging idea can be subtly shifted through repetition of more positive thoughts. At the end of each day, evaluate and reflect on your efforts. After completing three days of mantras, sum up your score against a possible total score of 15. Continue repeating these mantras to incorporate more lasting change.

Part 3: I CAN...

Chapter 9: ...Be Devoted

Day 1	Day 2	Day 3
1. I can detach myself from shame	2. I can learn from my peers	3. I can meditate
Score:	Score:	Score:
1. Failed x	1. Failed	1. Failed x
2. Poor	2. Poor	2. Poor
3. Fair	3. Fair x	3. Fair
4. Good	4. Good	4. Good
5. Excellent	5. Excellent	5. Excellent
1	3	1
Note: *I can't forgive myself for my failures.*	**Note:** *I have begun to reach out when I get stuck.*	**Note:** *I have a hard time to apply the right concentration.*

Total Possible Score: 15   My Score for Part 1, Section 1: 6 [sum of day 1 + day 2 + day 3]

CONCLUSION

LEARNING TO BE MORE RESILIENT, A DAILY PRACTICE

Now that you have read these profiles and absorbed their lessons, we ask that you consider again the story of Helen Keller's journey out of the dark and silence. Remember the story of Annie Sullivan, patiently spelling words into Helen Keller's palm while attempting to teach the connection to its corresponding object. We know that the letters w-a-t-e-r washed away darkness, as the world once again opened up to young Helen.

What few of us know is that, as Annie Sullivan added 30 new words to her pupil's vocabulary that day, along with subsequent hundreds in the years to come, she prefaced each with one very small word: "and."

For the 6-year old Helen, who lost both hearing and sight before her second birthday, the word "and" spelled possibility. Every moment opened up into an opportunity for grasping some new concept and for embracing a whole universe of hope. "And" also symbolized the connection to new friends, each time she added another to her circle of supporters.

Helen went on to finish high school. Then, Mark Twain had a hand in helping her attend

Radcliffe College by introducing her to Standard Oil magnate Henry Rogers, who footed the tuition bill. Though she struggled as a co-ed, isolated by her disabilities, Helen's network broadened once more "and" included John Macy. The Harvard professor would help Helen publish her memoirs in 1903 and she graduated with honors a year later.

In this way, she lengthened the chain of connections to Alexander Graham Bell, Charlie Chaplin, and every U.S. president from Grover Cleveland to Lyndon Johnson. Phillips Brooks taught Helen about spirituality. The Zoellner String Quartet introduced Helen to a world of music. Though profoundly deaf, Helen was able to place her fingers on the resonant wood of a table before her and feel the music and its measured rhythms: "and one, and two, and three, and four." The experience was transformative, allowing Helen yet one more glimpse into a world many of us do not give a second thought.

Indeed, Helen made a practice of stringing these friends and experiences into a great length of blessings, especially when she would weary of the time it took to read a few pages, knowing that other women could laugh, sing, and dance as they pleased. Though the

Zoellner Quartet's music prompted Helen to move in time to the vibrations she felt, dancing was a mystery to her until she met the maven of modern dance, Martha Graham.

The two became friends and it was not long before Helen started visiting the studio regularly, learning about movement through maintaining an exquisite sensitivity to the vibrations made by the dancers' feet sweeping across the floor and softly landing from jumps and turns. On occasion, Helen was so overcome by her desire to dance that she rose to her feet. The documentary "The Unconquered" has captured Helen swaying gently, her face suffused with delight, as Graham's dancers circle around her.

Another visit taught Helen the simple joy of jumping. Circling Merce Cunningham's waist with her hands, she feels the movement as he leaps up and lands over and over again.

Years later, in her autobiography, Martha Graham would recall those visits and recognize why they resonated so much. "The word "and" is inseparable from the dance, and leads us into most of the exercises and movements," she wrote. "It led her into the life of vibration. And her life enriched our studio. And to close the circle, all of our dance classes begin with the teacher saying, 'And...one!'"

"And" is a powerful principle of resilience. In its function as a conjunction in the English language it joins two distinct thoughts and binds them together in a sentence. It also allows space that the comma doesn't provide. In music, as in dance, the "and" is the space for preparation for a note, a phrase, a step or a turn. That room allows us to breathe and prepare, to reset and continue. It can mean the difference between slumping into submission, or smiling and shrugging off a setback.

In Japanese, the word to suggest that interval is *Ma*.

"It is best described as a consciousness of place, not in the sense of an enclosed three-dimensional entity, but rather the simultaneous awareness of form and non-form deriving from an intensification of vision."[32]

Ma is not something that is created by compositional elements; it is the thing that takes place in the imagination of the human who experiences these elements. Therefore *Ma* can be defined as experiential place understood with emphasis on interval."

Practicing meditation, we can use "and" or *Ma* to give rise to the inspiration that comes from imagining possibilities. Each time we pause to inhale *and* exhale is an opportunity to build hope out of darkness, an exercise in counting towards the light.

Building upon the concept of "and," you will want to consider each of the lessons we presented in the previous chapters in turn. As you begin to set your intention, preface the mantra with the word "and." If you can, speak it out loud or, just say it in your mind. Do this as if you were counting: and one, and two, and three, etc.

Invoking the word "and" before each intention expands the possibilities and creates a string of connections between the mantras that will eventually help you form a chain of resilience through core concepts. As always, we encourage you to keep repeating these powerful phrases to build an unshakeable mindset that may serve you well in times of trouble.

And with that, we invite you to begin becoming a more resilient you.

REFERENCES

1 Keller, Helen, and Anne M. Sullivan. *The Story of My Life*. Ed. John A. Macy. New York: Doubleday, 1905. *The Story of My Life*. UPenn. Web. 12 May 2015. <http://digital.library.upenn.edu/women/keller/life/life.html>.

2 "The Tale of Helen Keller." *Dichotomistic Logic*. Dichotomistic, 2006. Web. 12 May 2015. <http://www.dichotomistic.com/mind_readings_helen%20keller.html>.

3 "Professional Bio- Daniel Kish." *World Access for the Blind*. World Access for the Blind, n.d. Web. 12 May 2015. <http://www.worldaccessfortheblind.org/node/350>.

4 Grotberg, Edith H. *A Guide to Promoting Resilience in Children: Strengthening the Human Spirit*. N.p.: Bernard Van Leer Foundation, 1995. *A Guide to Promoting Resilience in Children: Strengthening the Human Spirit*. Resilience Net. Web. 12 May 2015. <http://resilnet.uiuc.edu/library/grotb95b.html>.

5 "Bleomycin (Injection Route)." Side Effects. Mayo Clinic, n.d. Web. 13 May 2015. <http://www.mayoclinic.org/drugs-supplements/bleomycin-injection-route/side-effects/drg-20067165>.

6 Sack, Andy. "Lessons I Learned from Having Cancer." *A Sack of Seattle*. N.p., 15 Jan. 2013. Web. 12 May 2015. <http://asackofseattle.com/blog/lessons-i-learned-from-having-cancer>.

7 Piff, Paul K., Daniel M. Stancato, Stéphane Côté, Rodolfo Mendoza-Denton, and Dacher Keltner. "Higher Social Class Predicts Increased Unethical Behavior." *Proceedings of the National Academy of Sciences of the United States of America*. Ed. Richard E. Nisbett. PNAS, 27 Feb. 2012. Web. 12 May 2015. <http://www.pnas.org/content/109/11/4086?tab=author-info>.

8 Williams, Andrew. "Power-crazed Bosses Are on the Rise: Psychologist Oliver James Explains Why." *Metro UK*. Metro, 04 Feb. 2014. Web. 12 May 2015. <http://metro.co.uk/2014/02/04/power-crazed-bosses-are-on-the-rise-psychologist-oliver-james-explains-why-4289507/>.

9 Duggan, Maeve. "Online Harassment." *Pew Research Center*. Pew Research Center, 22 Oct. 2014. Web. 12 May 2015. <http://www.pewinternet.org/2014/10/22/online-harassment/>.

10 Wainwright, Julie, and Angela Mohan, M.F.T. *ReBoot: My Five Life-Changing Mistakes and How I Have Moved On*. N.p.: urge, 2009. *Amazon*. Amazon.com, Inc., 15 Apr. 2009. Web. 13 May 2015. <http://www.amazon.com/ReBoot-Five-Life-Changing-Mistakes-Moved/dp/1439232555>

11 Goldman, David. "10 Big Dot.com Flops."

CNNMoney. Cable News Network, 10 Mar. 2010. Web. 12 May 2015. <http://money.cnn.com/galleries/2010/technology/1003/gallery.dot_com_busts/>.

12 Smith, Melinda, and Jeanne Segal. "Laughter Is the Best Medicine." *Helpguide.org*. Helpguide, Apr. 2015. Web. 12 May 2015. <http://www.helpguide.org/articles/emotional-health/laughter-is-the-best-medicine.htm>.

13 Dishman, Lydia. "Why We Can't Sleep And What It's Doing to Our Work." *Fast Company*. Fast Company, 05 May 2014. Web. 12 May 2015. <http://www.fastcompany.com/3029991/work-smart/why-we-cant-sleep-and-what-its-doing-to-our-work>.

14 Cohen, David. "Me.dium." Web log post. *Hi, I'm David G Cohen*. N.p., 31 Oct. 2006. Web. 12 May 2015. <http://www.davidgcohen.com/2006/10/31/medium---social-discovery-in-real-time/>.

15 Rao, Leena. "Walmart Acquires Mobile And Social Ad Targeting Startup OneRiot." *TechCrunch*. AOL Inc., 13 Sept. 2011. Web. 12 May 2015. <http://techcrunch.com/2011/09/13/walmart-acquires-mobile-and-social-ad-targeting-startup-oneriot/>.

16 Reynolds, Gretchen. "How Exercise May Protect Against Depression." *The New York Times*. The New York Times Company, 01 Oct. 2014. Web. 12 May 2015. <http://well.blogs.nytimes.com/2014/10/01/how-exercise-may-protect-against-depression/>.

17 Grotberg, Edith. Countering Depression with the

Five Building Blocks of Resilience. N.p.: National Educational Service, 1999. Countering Depression with the Five Building Blocks of Resilience - Edith H. Grotberg. Resilience Net. Web. 12 May 2015. <http://resilnet.uiuc.edu/library/grotb99.html>.

18 Fox, Jodie. "The Shoe Entrepreneur." Interview by Martine Harte. *Engaging Women*. Engaging Women, 03 Sept. 2014. Web. 12 May 2015. <http://engagingwomen.com.au/interviews/jodie-fox-shoes-of-prey/>.

19 O'Boyle, Ernest H., Jr., Ronald H. Humphrey, Jeffrey M. Pollack, Thomas H. Hawver, and Paul A. Story. "The Relation between Emotional Intelligence and Job Performance: A Meta-analysis." *Journal of Organizational Behavior* 32.5 (2011): 788-818. *Wiley Online Library*. John Wiley & Sons, Inc., 22 July 2010. Web. 12 May 2015. <http://onlinelibrary.wiley.com/doi/10.1002/job.714/abstract>.

20 Hölzel, Britta K., Sara W. Lazar, Tim Gard, Zev Schuman-Olivier, David R. Vago, and Ulrich Ott. *Perspectives on Psychological Science*. 6th ed. Vol. 6. N.p.: Sage Publications, 2011. *L.A. Dharma*. 19 Mar. 2012. Web. 12 May 2015. <http://ladharma.org/pdfs/lad-178.pdf>.

21 Kabat-Zinn, Jon. "Meeting Pain with Awareness." *Mindful*. Foundation for a Mindful Society, n.d. Web. 13 May 2015. <http://www.mindful.org/in-body-and-mind/mindfulness-based-stress-reduction/meeting-pain-with-awareness>.

22 "Patents by Assignee REVNETICS, INC." *Justia Patents Database*. Justia, n.d. Web. 13 May 2015. <http://patents.justia.com/assignee/revnetics-inc>.

23 "Revnetics." *CrunchBase*. Aol Inc., n.d. Web. 13 May 2015. <http://www.crunchbase.com/organization/revnetics>.

24 "Kamal Ravikant's Investors." *AngelList*. AngelList, n.d. Web. 13 May 2015. <https://angel.co/kamalravikant>.

25 Feld, Brad. "After Failure, What's Next?" Web log post. *Feld Thoughts*. Brad Feld, 19 June 2014. Web. 13 May 2015. <http://www.feld.com/archives/2014/06/failure-whats-next.html>.

26 "INTERLIANT INC (INIT) IPO Company Overview." *NASDAQ.com*. NASDAQ, n.d. Web. 13 May 2015. <http://www.nasdaq.com/markets/ipos/company/interliant-inc-9295-4702>.

27 WHIR Staff. "Interliant Announces Major Restructuring, Lays off 190 - Web Host Industry Review." *WHIR*. INET Interactive, 15 Mar. 2001. Web. 13 May 2015. <http://www.thewhir.com/web-hosting-news/interliant-announces-major-restructuring-lays-off-190>.

28 Nickel, Brad. "Interliant Knows When to Host 'em ...." *InternetNews.com*. QuinStreet Inc., 29 Oct. 2001. Web. 13 May 2015. <http://www.internetnews.com/xSP/article.php/912541/Interliant+Knows+When+to+Host+em+.htm>.

29 "IN RE I SUCCESSOR CORP." *Leagle*. Leagle, Inc,

n.d. Web. 13 May 2015. <http://www.leagle.com/decision/2005961321BR640_1890>.

30 Feld, Brad. "The Worse Way To Respond To 'Vomit Moments' Is With Fear." *Business Insider Australia*. Allure Media, 28 Aug. 2012. Web. 13 May 2015. <http://www.businessinsider.com.au/the-vomit-moment-2012-8>.

31 Mayo Clinic Staff. "Meditation: A Simple, Fast Way to Reduce Stress." *Mayo Clinic*. Mayo Foundation for Medical Education and Research, n.d. Web. 13 May 2015. <http://www.mayoclinic.org/tests-procedures/meditation/in-depth/meditation/art-20045858>.

32 Day, Andrea. "Ma- The Japanese Spatial Expression." *Buildings & Cities in Japanese History*. Columbia University, 1998. Web. 13 May 2015. <http://www.columbia.edu/itc/ealac/V3613/ma/>.

AUTHOR BIOS

About Faisal Hoque

Faisal Hoque is the founder of Shadoka and other companies. Shadoka enables entrepreneurship, growth, and social impact. Author of several books, including *"Everything Connects – How to Transform and Lead in the Age of Creativity, Innovation and Sustainability"* (McGraw Hill, 2014) and *"Survive to Thrive – 27 Practices of Resilient Entrepreneurs, Innovators, And Leaders" (Motivational Press, 2015)*.

Formerly with GE and other global brands, he regularly contributes to *Fast Company*, *Business Insider*, and *Huffington Post*. His work has also appeared in the *Wall Street Journal, BusinessWeek, Mergers & Acquisitions, Forbes*, and *Leadership Excellence* among other publications. American Management Association (AMA) named him one of the **Leaders to Watch in 2015**. The editors of Ziff-Davis Enterprise named him one of the **Top 100 Most Influential People in Technology** alongside leading entrepreneurs such as Steve Jobs, Bill Gates, Michael Dell, Larry Page, and others. Trust Across America -Trust Around the World (TAA-TWA) named him one of the **Top 100 Thought**

Leaders alongside global leaders such as Bill George, Tony Hsieh, Doug Conant, Howard Schultz, and others.

Faisal Hoque is a frequent public speaker at entrepreneurship conferences, innovation forums, business schools, and leadership summits. His talks are focused on entrepreneurship, innovation, creativity, leadership, mindfulness, and social impact.

Follow him @faisal_hoque or visit faisalhoque.com.

About Lydia Dishman

Lydia Dishman learned about the power of resilience from an early age. As an infant, she spent months in the foster care system in New York City before being adopted by a large, loving Italian family in the Bronx. She credits their stability and support as the foundation from which she was able to build a life of opportunity.

Lydia has enjoyed a long career as an independent journalist, contributing to both print and online publications for the past 15 years. Her work has appeared in a variety of publications including *Fast Company*, *CBS MoneyWatch*, *Entrepreneur Magazine*, *Popular Science*, *Forbes*, *The Guardian*, *Slate*, and the *New York Times' T Magazine*, among others.

CPSIA information can be obtained
at www.ICGtesting.com
Printed in the USA
BVHW061002011218
534524BV00003B/502/P